D1091008

Development and Change in Highland Yemen

Abandoned terraces, highlands of Yemen.

Development and Change in Highland Yemen

Charles F. Swagman

University of Utah Press
Salt Lake City
1988

Library of Congress Cataloging-in-Publication Data

Swagman, Charles F., 1952-
   Development and change in highland Yemen.

   Bibliography: p.
   Includes index.
   1. Rural development—Yemen—Case studies.
2. Villages—Yemen—Case studies.   I. Title.
HN664.Z9C678   1988   307.1'4'095332   88–20603
ISBN 0–87480–295–4

To Fatima, Martine, and Zuhra

Contents

ILLUSTRATIONS

PHOTOGRAPHS

TABLES

Preface

Oftentimes the circumstances of doing field research in a developing nation have as much impact on the final outcome as any well-laid research plans and designs. Initially, this project began as an anthropological study of diffusion and innovation, investigating the consequences of the recent introduction of Western or "cosmopolitan" medicine in a very traditional region of rural Yemen. The original plan entailed a study of development, but at a much more narrowly focused level than is addressed in this book. I intended to study first-hand the kind of cultural changes brought about by the introduction of a novel technology and belief system into a traditional environment. Thus, an isolated, relatively undeveloped region that was just completing its first health center was chosen as a field site. But unforeseen circumstances required that I abandon this project in midstream and concentrate on the wider issues of local development.

The community, Kusma, in the Jibal Rayma region of the western central highlands of Yemen, is nestled on a lofty ridge under the shadow of two mountain peaks, Jabal Barad and Jabal Kusma, and had a commanding view of the Tihama plains, some eight thousand feet below. No roads led to the community, accessible only by a grueling seven- to ten-hour hike. The trail, which starts in the steamy, humid tropical wadis of the Tihama, crosses sun-baked lower foothills, ascends slopes so steep that stairways with over two thousand steps have been laid out for pack animals, and finally ends in the cool breezes of the mountain ridge. The relative isolation of Kusma made it the ideal field location, and it was my home for the better part of two years.

Although not exactly warm and friendly, the people seemed accepting and tolerant of my presence. However, underneath the idyllic "Shangri-la" surface, many political tensions were boiling. Prior to my arrival in Yemen, I made the acquaintance of a professor at Sanaᶜa University, a personal friend of the paramount shaykh of Jibal Rayma, who provided me with a letter of introduction. I arrived with a personal escort and an official letter of introduction from the Yemen Center for Research and Study and a place was immediately found for me to live. The accommodation was a single room on the top floor of an old house in the center of the community on the fringe of the marketplace.

I began my stay by attending the daily sessions with the director of the district, primarily because it seemed proper to introduce myself to the authorities and because it was the focus of most public activity in the community. It was also a good place to practice my Arabic and to pick up the local dialect. Invitations to other villages and hamlets were soon extended to me as a result of contacts made at the director's office, and more systematic ethnographic data collecting began.

Local leaders began to befriend me. However, I was the first Westerner to spend any significant time in the community, so my presence was seen by some as suspicious. Additionally, political tensions were beginning to foment in the region, so I was specifically asked by a delegation of local leaders not to conduct any house-to-house surveys or a census and not to take notes publicly. Since all of these were integral to my original plans, I had to abandon my initial research design, which included a detailed network analysis.

Tolerated, but not really accepted, my presence in the community was marginal, and I was frequently described as someone studying the language and history and occasionally as someone interested in local customs. My identity varied, since no one could quite understand what a social scientist was, and I was often thought of as some kind of "agent" or investigator (*mubahith*). I tried explaining that I was a student interested in studying their traditions and customs, particularly folk medicine (*it-tibb ish-sha*ᶜ*bi*), and this was satisfying to some. Initially, my questions were focused primarily on medicine, and I began by collecting samples of medicinal plants. However, soon by happenstance it became known that I could repair diesel generators, and because these recently introduced machines frequently broke down, I became known as the *muhandis* (engineer) of the region. After struggling five months, I was finally able to serve a useful purpose. These skills carried me into many more households and into more outlying regions than would otherwise have been possible in my vague "investigator" role. I developed a reputation as the best mechanic and electrician of the region and was accepted by the community. On more than a few occasions, I was strongly urged to convert to Islam, marry a local girl, and settle down.

Despite its status as a less-developed country, the cost of living in Yemen is extremely high. I adopted a migrant life-style that was typical of many of the young men of the community. On two occasions, I had to find employment in order to continue to finance my studies. Short contracts were completed with the American Peace Corps in Sana°a and with the German government. The latter involved conducting a household survey on fuelwood consumption in the Haraz region. These activities broadened my experiences in Yemen and gave me the opportunity to become familiar with social and economic conditions in other regions in Yemen. Each of them allowed my studies in Jibal Rayma to continue, since my original research money had long run out.

By living and working in the community for about two years, I eventually became privy to some of the local disputes and problems, especially in regard to the local development association, and I won the confidence of a few key informants. The situation seemed to be improving, though it took much longer than anticipated, and I finally was formally allowed to begin conducting my survey (semistructured interviews) in villages outside the district center.

Then, in December 1981, the political situation erupted. The National Democratic Front, a leftist-oriented movement in opposition to the government in Sana°a, began a series of raids and assassination attempts that created a sense of fear and disorganization in the region. Despite my long-term work in the community, many people began to reinterpret my presence in terms of the political turmoil. Few knew where "the front" was located or who its members were, but widespread fear of it made travel and research impossible. After being shaken from my sleep by an air attack and hearing a hysterical neighbor woman shouting at me that it was all my fault, I decided that my presence in the community would place those who had befriended me in unnecessary jeopardy and left the community with the hope of resuming research in another area.

By this time, my research funds had again run out; fortunately, I had previously been recruited to work for a health program in Dhamar province sponsored by the Netherlands government. Many of their project needs overlapped with my personal research interests and I seized upon this opportunity to continue my research under the sponsorship of this program. Because the project area, Anis, bordered Jibal Rayma, I felt that little would be lost by continuing work there. The front activities limited travel in this region as well, but it was not as dangerous, and I began developing contacts in the community of Dawran, a district center somewhat similar to Kusma. This field location was not nearly as isolated and was accessible by a rather good road system. As an employee of the project, my personal research interests were secondary to the dictates of the program, which were primarily action-oriented. Part of my responsibility was to establish working relationships with those involved in local development, and particularly to do some public relations work, explaining the objectives of the project to the people. However, after a solid foundation for research in Dawran Anis was established, tragic events prevented me from even beginning. The devastating earthquake of December 12, 1982, completely destroyed the community of Dawran, killing about fifteen hundred people and leaving hundreds of thousands of people in the region at least temporarily homeless. The initially planned research was never completed.

Nevertheless, as a result of my long-term and intimate association with the two areas, Jibal Rayma and Anis, I was able to collect basic socioeconomic and sociopolitical data that have gone into the development of this book. These two neighboring areas contrasted dramatically in the success of their efforts at local development, and this presented a natural problem. I began to ask myself: why was Anis so successful while Jibal Rayma was not? That question has become the main focus of this study.

A comment should be made on the quality and quantity of information presented here. As an ethnographer, part of my field technique was to record as much information as possible about all facets of life in these regions. Data were gathered through extensive participant observation. However, since the topic is not that which was initially planned, gaps in my notes inevitably appeared. I have attempted to fill these by searching the published sources, such as other ethnographic studies and central government statistical reports. Particularly difficult to obtain were hard economic and production data. Although the Yemenis are very eager to ask how much one's salary is, they are very reluctant to give any but the most generalized statements about their own financial affairs. Nevertheless, a reasonable idea about the economic status of the people was obtainable by observing the kind of consumer spending they engaged in and the quality of their houses and by paying attention to some of the more subtle cues about financial status (such as the type of home furnishing and the quality of the *janbiya*—a decorative curved dagger worn by adult men—and other elements of personal dress). Other economic indicators were drawn from calculations based on published sources. Additionally, many of the gaps that were uncovered during the writing of this book have been filled through correspondence with key informants.

Acknowledgments

This research was initially funded through a Fulbright-Hays fellowship (1979–80), grant number 600–79–02938. The maps (TPC K6A) reproduced in this book are published by the Defense Mapping Agency, protected under Her Majesty's Stationery Office Crown Copyright, and are used by permission.

During the four years of living and working in Yemen (January 1980 through December 1983), a number of people and institutions extended their hospitality and support. The Yemen Center for Research and Study, Sana‘a, which is the official sponsor of all researchers in Yemen, was most helpful in providing letters of introduction and in dealing with the necessary clearances. Without the cooperation and hospitality of a number of friends in the capital city Sana‘a, my stay in Yemen would have been much shorter and far less interesting. I would like to thank James Callahan (cultural attaché, U.S. Embassy, Sana‘a), Rick Carboni, Dr. Richard Verdary, Jon Bjørnsson, Zohra Merabit, and Barbara Croken for lending assistance and providing accommodations on my trips into the town. The discussions of *al-lajna al-faniya fil qa‘*, a group of close friends who gathered each Thursday to chew qat in Sana‘a were a stimulating source of information; this book is, in a sense, an epiphenomenon of the efforts of this group. During my period of employment with the Dhamar Governorate Health Services Program, a number of colleagues provided much-needed assistance in data collection. Muhammad Khawani, Yahiya idh-Dhari, my assistant ‘Abdul Rahman Kalaz, and Dr. Fatima Zuhra Kasarat provided translations and explanations of aspects of Yemeni social organization.

To the people of Anis and Jibal Rayma, I also wish to extend my warmest regards and heartfelt appreciation for their hospitality. Among the many friends I made, who are too numerous to list, I would like to give particular recognition to Muhammad ʿAbdullah al-Fadli for his excellent assistance in helping me to understand the affairs of the local development association in Anis and for his correspondence, which helped me answer many questions left unresolved during the fieldwork. Hydar ʿAli Naagi of Khudar, Kusma, Jibal Rayma, was a consistently gracious host and by extending his friendship made it all possible. Hydar's keen interest in history and social science was of the utmost value. To these, and to all those I have omitted, I extend my gratitude.

I would like to thank Dr. Richard Tutwiler for reading earlier drafts and suggesting the importance of power relations in Yemen and their influence on local development, and my mother Loraine for proofreading some of the drafts. Finally, I would like to express my greatest appreciation to Dr. John G. Kennedy, who first introduced me to Yemen and provided extraordinary support throughout my graduate studies at UCLA.

A NOTE ON TRANSLITERATION

In this book I have elected to anglicize the most common Arabic words and to add an *s* to the singular to make the plural. The names of places and people have been rendered in their most usual spellings. In accordance with University of Utah Press style, diacritical markings and differentiation of emphatic letters such as sin and sad are omitted; only the ʿayn and hamza are retained as separate characters. While this may inconvenience some readers, confusion over transliteration should not present a significant problem because the number of Arabic terms used in this book has been kept to a minimum.

Development and Change in Highland Yemen

1

Introduction

This book is about local development in the western central highlands of North Yemen, a small, mountainous country located on the southwestern corner of the Arabian Peninsula. In 1962, a military coup d'etat overthrew the remains of a thousand-year-old Zaydi Imamate (religious kingdom) and set the stage for emergence of the Yemen Arab Republic. Embroiled in a protracted civil war and internal political strife, the country had no possibility of successful socioeconomic development until 1970, after cessation of the hostilities between the republican and royalist forces. Thus, local rural development in Yemen is a historically recent phenomenon and eminently suited for first-hand observation and study.

In this study the term "local development" refers primarily to the processes of basic infrastructure building in rural Yemen. Prior to the revolution, there were only a few hundred kilometers of passable roads in the entire country, modern health facilities were virtually nonexistent, and formal education was only available in the larger towns (Hoogstraal and Kuntz 1952:213–245). In the postrevolutionary period, infrastructure building (particularly roads, schools, health care facilities, and electrification and water projects) has been the main concern in the rural areas. Parallels can be drawn between the approach to local-level rural development that predominates in rural Yemen, with its focus on infrastructure building, and the recent "basic needs" approach to development advocated by the international development community (Streeten 1977:8; Combs 1980:11; Lee 1981:107; Cohen 1984:423). In these approaches to development, a greater emphasis is placed on improving the rural quality of life than on achieving typically economic objectives such as increasing per capita production.

Since the 1962 revolution, demands for improvements in basic infrastructure have increased, far outstripping the central government's ability to supply the necessary assistance, especially in the mountainous rural areas. In fact, when central government services are used as an index for development, Yemen is one of the poorest of the less-developed countries. Recognizing its inability to do much for the rural hinterland during the mid-1970s, the central government adopted a strategy that actively encouraged local initiative development. This policy emerged as an amplification of an earlier grass-roots self-help movement. During the civil war period (1962–70), some locally organized welfare institutions expanded their range of activities from assisting the poor and needy to providing relief for families and villages severely damaged by the war and aiding in village-level reconstruction efforts. The seeds of the local development movement were sown during this period. In the early 1970s, formal state recognition was given to these first local development associations (Cohen et al. 1981:1043).

During the presidency of Ibrahim al-Hamdi (1974–77), the local development associations (LDAs) were successful in obtaining control of traditional agricultural taxes (*zakat*), which enabled the LDAs further to expand their range of activities. The late president's policies resulted in the expansion of the number of legally chartered LDAs from 29 in 1973 to a high of 191 by 1979.[1] Since the early 1970s, the LDAs have been the principal agencies for local-level rural development.

This study focuses on the efforts of the people in the rural western central highlands region, who, recognizing their needs for facilities and services, have attempted to coordinate efforts at rural development through a system of local organizations. The Yemen local development movement is an example of innovative approaches that are occurring with greater frequency in the developing countries.

DEVELOPMENT STRATEGIES

Recently, analysis of alternative development strategies has focused on the basic inputs to rural development—whether they are generated at the local level or at the administrative centers. The contrast most often drawn is between development "from above" and development "from below" (Pitt 1976; Stohr and Taylor 1981). Development from below is best understood when contrasted with the approach that has been the mainstay of governments, development agencies, and international organizations for the past half-century:

> Development "from above" has its roots in neoclassical economic theory and its spatial manifestation is the growth centre concept. . . . The basic hypothesis is that development is driven by external demand and innovation impulses, and that from a few dynamic sectoral or geographic clusters, development would, either in a spontaneous or induced way, "trickle down" to the rest of the system. Such strategies, as well as being outward-looking or externally oriented, have tended to be urban and industrial in nature, capital intensive, and dominated by high technology and a "large project" approach. (Stohr and Taylor 1981:1)

One need only glance at the Middle East to see the predominance of this rural development strategy, the Sudanese Gezira scheme being perhaps the most salient example (Barnett 1977).

In contrast, development from below reflects the trend to reevaluate the nature and purpose of development (Seers 1969; Wiarda 1983):

> Development "from below" considers development to be based primarily on maximum mobilization of each area's natural, human, and institutional resources with the primary objective being the satisfaction of the basic needs of the inhabitants of that area. . . . There is an inherent distrust of the "trickle down" or spread effect expectations of past development policies. Development "from below" strategies are basic-needs oriented, labour-intensive, small-scale, regional-resource-based, and argue for the use of "appropriate" rather than "highest technology." (Stohr and Taylor 1981:2)

By harnessing local resources, it is possible to retain the local community as the focus of development efforts.

Development from below represents a type of collective activity that in and of itself has probably always been a part of human history. Certainly, the anthropological literature is replete with case studies of collective activities such as work bees, farms, hunting parties, and the like. As early as the writings of Ruth Benedict, anthropologists have been interested in these examples of social synergy (Mead 1959). Development from below differs from earlier conceptions and could be seen as emerging as a new development paradigm in that these kinds of self-help activities are taking on formal dimensions within state administrative systems.[2] The Yemen local development associations have grown from a handful of ad hoc self-help organizations into legally chartered administrative entities with active support at the national level.

The development strategy of the Yemen organizations is a combination of local financing, planning, and implementation with a significant central government input in the areas of policy, planning, and financing. The Yemen case is a unique mixture of development from above and development from below.[3]

David Pitt has suggested that adequate development theory is still dependent on case studies of development that "allow for situational explanations of the dynamics of development complexity in time and space" (1976b:1).[4] One of the strengths of the anthropological approach to the study of social processes is a "holistic" perspective that attempts to take into account historical, economic, ecological, and sociocultural variables within a given time framework. Therefore, anthropological case studies are in their very nature "situational."[5] Given such a broad perspective, anthropological research results and methods are often interdisciplinary; this study, with its purposefully eclectic orientation, follows this tradition.

THE PROBLEM

In an extensive cross-cultural survey of local development organizations including cooperatives, credit associations, and local development associations, Esman and Uphoff (1984) report quite a range of successes and failures in attempts at rural development undertaken through local organizations. Their research suggests the need for studies that may indicate why certain local organizations are successful and others are not. The case of the local development associations in Yemen offers an opportunity to address precisely this type of question.

This book is an account of dramatic differences in the relative successes in local development in two sections of the western central highlands region of Yemen. The contrasts in local development are surprising, given the fact that they emerged among people sharing the same agrarian peasant culture patterns and living in the same mountainous environment. The aims of this book are at once comparative and descriptive; it seeks to uncover a range of factors that were important in the process of rural development while also providing detailed description of the way rural development is conceived of and executed in rural Yemen. Rural development is a complex process, so it is important to assess the relative importance of the myriad of variables that come into play. Although it is beyond the scope of a comparative analysis of two cases to form any generalized conclusions about specific key factors, it is possible to explore how the processes of local development unfold within a specific space and time.

THE RESEARCH STRATEGY:
THE COMPARATIVE APPROACH

The most common purpose of social science research is to seek verification of theoretical propositions through systematic analysis of a body of data—to state a thesis and attempt to prove it. Often, however, the basic theoretical paradigms are weak or in crisis (Kuhn 1970), and the social scientist is prompted to seek alternative modes of analysis. Glasser and Strauss argue that another legitimate mode of analysis is the "discovery of theory from data—systematically obtained and analyzed in social research," that is, the generation of "grounded theory" (1967:1). One frequently employed strategy is to adopt a comparative methodology that involves the systematic choice and study of several comparison groups. In this procedure, a range of variables that the researcher deems relevant to the immediate problem can be systematically compared and associations can be noted. In the second phase of the generation of grounded theory, these associations may be more formally arranged into theoretical propositions and verified in other settings. In sociocultural anthropology, particularly in ethnology, such a method of controlled comparison has a long history, especially in research concerned with the middle range of theory (Merton 1949:5; Glasser and Strauss 1967:33).

The advantage provided by the comparative method is that, in the absence of the regulated conditions of the laboratory environment (typical of most social science field studies), some degree of control is still obtainable (Eggan 1954:759). However, some of the more serious difficulties in employing the comparative method involve defining units that can logically be compared and controlling for extraneous factors. In this regard, it has been suggested that a regional approach may significantly reduce the problem of uncontrolled influences (Eggan 1954:755). Comparative studies, especially in the social

sciences, are too often subject to criticism because they try to compare units that are essentially incomparable. One of the major meth-
odological difficulties is the definition of the units for comparison.
Regional analysis offers one solution to the problem:

> The point of defining regional systems . . . is to allow reasonable kinds
> of comparisons between equivalent units; any regional system can be
> broken down to a particular hierarchical level; systems at a given hier-
> archical level become the standard units of comparison.
>
> The standardization of comparative units is one obvious contribu-
> tion of regional analysis, necessary for comparative analysis of any social
> phenomena—social as well as geographical. Unless one is concerned
> with the comparative study of individuals, one must make comparison
> of social units as they exist within a spatial-territorial context; and unless
> the social unit is properly specified in this regard, comparison will be
> useless. (Smith 1976:10)

Thus, a regional approach provides some assurances that the units
of analysis share a basic common background and their comparison
is meaningful. In this study, the local development associations and
the local sociopolitical structures (e.g., descent groups, tribal segments, administrative units, etc.) exist within a specific spatial-
territorial context. Consequently, they constitute clearly defined units
that may be meaningfully compared. A regional frame has been
adopted in this study because it is a level of social organization larger
than the individual community, but smaller than the nation/state.
It is a level at which: (1) the processes of rural development are organized by the people, and (2) differences can be readily observed. A
second reason for adopting a regional approach is that it has been
noted that development from below is often articulated within a
regional context:

> The basic objective of development from below is the full development
> of a region's natural resources and human skills . . . initially for the
> satisfaction in equal measure of the basic needs of all of the regional or
> natural population, and subsequently for development objectives beyond
> this. Most basic needs services are territorially organized, and manifest
> themselves most intensely at the level of small scale social groups and
> local or regional communities. (Stohr 1981:43)

Since a significant portion of rural development in highland Yemen
is implemented through local development associations that are organized at the various regional administrative levels, analysis above the

level of the standard anthropological monograph on a small community is appropriate.

Having defined the region and the units of comparison, the first step in any comparative analysis is to look for common factors whose effects can be identified and removed from the analysis; the purpose of a controlled comparison is to try and simplify the problem by holding constant as many underlying factors as possible, thereby reducing the number of possibly significant variables. Ecological, recent historical, and economic factors all have significant potential to affect the resource base necessary for rural development (Epstein 1962). Therefore, the first step in this analysis of local development is to compare the resource bases and the relative costs of development activities in the two areas, factoring out as many similarities as possible. Once the common factors have been controlled, a more detailed examination of the significant differences between the units of analysis may be possible. In short, the strength of the controlled comparison methodology is that it provides a means of isolating factors associated with successful rural development as well as factors associated with unsuccessful development, while allowing the common variables to be eliminated from the discussion. However, with a careful comparison of only two case studies, caution must be exercised in generalizing the findings beyond the sample. Nevertheless, comparative studies have value in that they contribute to the generation of grounded theory.

THE REGION

The western central highlands of Yemen are a region of very high, steep mountains that jut abruptly from the lowland Tihama plains. These mountains are carved by deep gorges and valleys or wadis that channel the runoff from the often violent afternoon thunderstorms. The climate is moderate, although the highest altitudes occasionally approach freezing during the winter months. Precipitation is between 400 and 600 millimeters per year, in the form of intense rain and hail. The entire region is subject to occasional drought.

The highland mountain areas support a peasantry based primarily on dry-land farming carried out on terraced slopes. In the lower elevations on the exposed, hot, and marginal lands—and especially in the tropical, humid wadis—live small groups of the very poor camped along the streambeds and in caves, who eke out an existence herding small flocks, working as day laborers, or, more often, selling tea and food to travelers making the journey from the lowland markets to the highland farms. The western central highlands are topographically distinct from the highlands plains region, as well as from the lowland Tihama. The western central highlands form an area with internal cultural and geographical similarities and with marked differences that separate it from surrounding areas.

The research for this book was conducted in a corridor through the western central highlands extending from Jibal Rayma in the west to the central plateau of Dhamar. Specifically, this study focuses on the area located within the latitudes of 14°30′ and 14°50′ north and longitudes 43°30′ and 44°30′ east. The region extends from the high plateau to the fringes of the lowland Tihama and, generally speaking, is a slice through the middle of the country (see map 1).

Within the western central highlands regional frame, the basic administrative unit of analysis in this study is the *qada′*, which best translates as subprovince. The two *qada′*'s in this study are Anis and Jibal Rayma.

Qada′ Anis

Qada′ Anis is comprised of three districts or *nahiya*s, Ma°bar-Jahran, Dawran, and Jabal ish-Shirq. The area covers 205,000 hectares, extending from the western edge of the central plains to the Jibal Rayma massif in the west and bounded on the north by Wadi Siham and on the south by Wadi Bani Muhammad and Maghrib °Ans. With a population of around 110,000, Anis has a density of 47.6 people per square kilometer (Swiss Technical Cooperation 1977).

Anis is predominantly a mountainous area, although it does contain some plains, most notably Qa° Jahran, Qa° al-Haql, and Qa° Bakil. The upper reaches of Wadi Rima° are prime agricultural lands that support intensive cereal farming as well as coffee and citrus. In the western areas of Anis, the mountain slopes become much more radical, and agriculture is limited to steep terraced hillsides.

Qada′ Jibal Rayma

Qada′ Jibal Rayma borders Anis on the west. Jibal Rayma is an isolated mountain range that is composed of five *nahiya*s: al-Jabin, as-Salafiya, Bilad it-Ta°am, al-Ja°fariya, and Kusma. The area is clearly defined by Wadi Siham in the north, the Tihama plain to the west, and Wadi Rima^c to the south (see map 1). A rugged mountainous region, Jibal Rayma covers 152,000 hectares (Revri 1983:115), with approximately 161,000 people. The population density is approximately 103 per square kilometer (Swiss Technical Cooperation 1977).

The location of Jibal Rayma favors intensive agriculture because it is one of the first mountains to catch the rainfall from storms blowing in from the Red Sea. In the dry season, the western slopes get a heavy afternoon cloud cover that produces conditions favorable for qat and coffee production.[6] The moisture carried on the winds from the Red Sea is also sufficient to support natural grasslands in the upper elevations, and there is ample natural fodder for sheep and goats. The area is intensively cultivated, but almost entirely on terraces. Only a limited amount of land in the *qada'* is in the Tihama plains region and in the major drainage systems of Wadi Siham and Wadi Rima^c. The Jibal Rayma people are highlanders who live in one of the most verdant regions in all Yemen.

PERSPECTIVES ON SOCIOPOLITICAL ORGANIZATIONS AND DEVELOPMENT

In the literature on social organization and development, considerable attention has been focused on the abilities of local social organizations, often characterized as based on "vertical" types of social relationships, to form appropriate social foundations for development programs. In analyzing the cooperative movement in Kenya, Widstrand (1972) has described vertical ties as those social relationships that cut across economic class boundaries. He includes precisely the kinds of traditional social groups found in rural Yemen as examples of traditional organizations based on such vertical relations.

> The horizontal relationships are relationships between people in the same economic position, while the vertical relationships are between individuals in various positions of economic power, either informal relationships such as patron-client relationships or dependent relationships such as creditor-debtor relationships or formal relationships, i.e., individuals belonging to the same cultural group, clan, lineage or family. (1972:18–19)

Other research on local development has questioned the importance of sociopolitical institutions based on vertical ties in the overall process of development. At issue is whether or not these kinds of organizations are a benefit or a hindrance (Dore 1971:60). One perspective holds that societies whose local-level sociopolitical organizations are based primarily on vertical types of social relations are highly susceptible to factionalism and localization of interests and thus make wide-scale cooperation difficult. In a general review of rural cooperatives, Worsley argues that social entities based on vertical ties, such as tribe or sect, rarely prove conducive to the development of cooperatives based on rational economic or managerial policies: "Traditional ties of kinship and neighborhood, caste and ethnicity too often work against the requirements of strict economic rationality. Established solidarities, that is, may be dysfunctional for the cooperatives rather than a social foundation on which modern cooperatives can be based" (1971:23–24). This position has also been noted by Carroll (1971), who, in a cross-cultural evaluation of rural development cooperatives, cites a number of studies that indicate that sociopolitical systems based on vertical ties are not well adapted to the type of cooperation necessary for modern cooperatives (see Carroll 1971:218; Crocombe 1971:196; Widstrand 1972:21).

In the literature on traditional organizations and development in the Middle East, Barakat also sees traditional social organization in terms of the division between horizontal and vertical loyalties: "Underdeveloped societies (such as Middle Eastern Arab countries) are characterized by religious, ethnic, regional, kinship and other forms of vertical loyalties that overshadow and undermine horizontal or social class loyalties. . . . In these traditional societies, the kinship, religious, regional and ethnic systems constitute the basic patterns of social organization" (1977:668). He also argues that these kinds of vertical loyalties severely limit the possibilities for modernization and development:

> So far as direct relationships between traditional ties and development are concerned, a number of empirical studies show that integration into kinship, religious and regional systems correlates negatively with modernism . . . to be more specific, integration into traditional institutions is likely to hinder development in the following ways: first, it makes for low rate of circulation of elites, leaders or decision makers . . . in short, traditional societies do not allow for emergence of new leadership. . . . Second, traditional loyalties have contributed to fragmentation on the local community level as well as on the country and national levels.

On the local community level, loyalties to competing traditional leaders, families and sects have prevented (1) extension of basic services as roads, electricity, water, etc.; (2) open and extensive dialogue between the different groups and factions. On the country level, kinship, religious and communal loyalties have contributed to rivalries and groupings that directly conflict with the broader interests of the country and retard its modernization. . . . (Barakat 1977:669–672)

Vertical sociopolitical groupings, which are in essence parochial, limit the possibilities for wide-scale cooperation because they encourage factionalism, restrict leadership to a limited set of powerful elites, and do not foster an attitude of cooperation that extends beyond the traditional social group.

In contrast to the argument that social groups based on vertical ties are detrimental to development are studies that identify features of traditional organizations that are conducive to large-scale cooperation and serve as springboards for development. Seibel and Massing's (1974) study of cooperatives in Liberia and the much-heralded Cornell Vicos project in Peru (Dobyns, Doughty, and Lasswell 1971) have demonstrated that systems based on vertical ties may be well adapted to the development of modern cooperatives. Traditional work groups, ethics that stress cooperation and group solidarity, and patterns of leadership emphasizing the importance of personal achievement have been features of traditional organizations associated with successful attempts to form cooperatives.

In the Middle East, there is also a divergence of opinions on the utility of groupings based on tribal or sectarian ties in the process of development. Citing case studies from Lebanon, which have been the basis for most analyses of the relationships between traditional sociopolitical groupings and development, Khalaf (1972) has challenged the assertion that traditional forms of organization based on vertical ties (such as family, tribe, and sect) are impediments to development. In a study of family firms, kinship associations, confessional bureaucracies, parochial voluntary associations, company unions, and political bosses (*za^{c}im*), Khalaf concludes that "the so-called traditional agencies and groupings have been instrumental in generating change and absorbing imbalances" and suggests that there are "several instances in which Lebanese traditions have had a reinforcing rather that retarding effect on development" (1972:571–73). Among the positive functions, he notes that these organizations have served as tension-reducing and integrative social mechanisms as well as being "functionally significant as innovative agents" (1972:574). In an analysis of the political importance of religious sects in Lebanon, Khouri (1972) has also noted that this form of sociopolitical organization had a positive influence on development as a basis for identification with social units larger than the immediate family or village.

Sociopolitical groups based on vertical ties, such as tribes, often have an articulated ideology that prescribes social relations. These can be powerful forces, charged with moral sentiment, for eliciting cooperation. Bardeleben's analysis of the cooperative movement in the Sudan concludes that ideological features of tribal social organization, particularly traditional cooperative activities (*nafir, faza*), formed the base for the modern cooperatives: "The modern cooperative system is also based on the same principles of mutual assistance underlying this traditional form of cooperative. It would seem that the given social structures promote the intelligibility and familiarity of the cooperative idea among the participants and greatly facilitate the development of modern cooperatives" (1973:89).

This perspective argues that traditional social groupings, such as the tribe and sectarian groups, which crosscut economic class boundaries, may have a positive effect on development in that they often serve to unite small, atomistic groups into larger sociopolitical entities that may be used as the social basis on which to develop cooperatives. Furthermore, this position makes note of the fact that values that encourage group solidarity, cooperation, and mutual benefit are often closely associated with traditional sociopolitical organization. Proponents of this position argue that such groups may, with some technical and managerial input, be transformed into modern cooperative institutions, since they are to some extent already incipient corporate groups.

Both positions are argued on the basis of case studies, and each has presented data to support its claims, making generalized conclusions difficult to assess. One of the main problems is that the arguments do not form a very coherent debate. Pitt (1976*a*) has pointed out that one of the main problems is that the frames of reference of case studies are often so different that comparisons become muddled. For example, the different perspectives on the Lebanese example are to some extent a result of the fact that each analyst has chosen a different social frame (i.e., national, regional, local, family, etc.) to analyze the problem. The kinds of solidarity attributed to sect- and kin-based associations by Khouri (1972) and Khalaf (1972) on a regional level are seen by Barakat (1977) on a national level as disintegrating and dysfunctional for development. Additionally, as the Lebanese situation tragically continues to demonstrate, groups that can unite for development purposes can also unite in conflict and destruction.

The tendency is to view the two perspectives as intrinsically opposed. Often it is argued that social institutions based on vertical ties, such as the tribe, inhibit the formation of class consciousness, thus constituting a barrier to development (Barakat 1977:668–70). However, the evidence from Yemen suggests that they need not be at odds and that classes may emerge within a system in which vertical loyalties are important.

Problems also result from the differences in types of traditional organizations and cooperative activities that are lumped into single categories. Although of some analytical usefulness, distinctions such as horizontal and vertical are also problematic in that they mask the very distinctive and often important differences between traditional systems. Tribe and sect share certain features that crosscut economic class boundaries, but they are quite distinct social forms, with different principles of organization, recruitment, and responsibilities. Furthermore, the interests of classes may be the same as the interests of tribes and sects and exist together without conflict.

Additionally, the types of cooperative activities included in the arguments above are quite variable, including collectivized production schemes, communal farms and factories, marketing cooperatives, and self-help infrastructure-building organizations. These problems make the generalized conclusions of Barakat (1977) and Worsley (1971) difficult to support. Nevertheless, the basic question of the relationship between traditional forms of social organization and development (Dore 1971:60) remains open and of interest. Yemen, a country in which tribalism is still active but is also undergoing rapid socioeconomic change with the emergence of new classes, is well suited to an analysis of social and political relations and their influence on local development.

The Argument

Local development requires a corporate ability to marshal and allocate both locally and externally generated resources. In this environment of competition for scarce resources, it is argued that local-level rural development is particularly vulnerable to social and political forces. This study demonstrates that there is significant regional variability in sociopolitical organization in the two *qada's* that affects the ability to achieve sustained levels of cooperation. Significant differences can be noted both at the ideological level and at a more materialist level. On the ideological level, there are cultural rationales for community action, and these are related to four aspects of social organization: kinship, tribal membership, sectarian allegiance, and obligations resulting from residence in a defined area. Furthermore, the ideology of cooperation associated with each of these four areas forms a gestalt; when all four are present, the potential for cooperative action is greatest. Local development requires community action, collective decision making, and a general spirit of cooperation. It is argued that, when ideological factors are examined, a higher degree of cooperation was generated in Anis due to the presence of all four aspects of local social organization. In contrast, it is shown that Jibal Rayma lacked a sense of tribal organization; consequently, the ability to invoke the tribal ideology of unity as a force in generating community action was absent.

The variations in social organization in the two areas are also associated with significantly different constellations of power—the types and levels of power yielded to community leaders (e.g., persuasion, coercion, economic leveraging, etc.), their ability to regulate local public affairs, and their power to harness outside resources. Power differences can also be detected at a group level, as exemplified by sectarian competition. It is argued that the power structures in the two cases, together with variations in social organization and ideological factors, explain the differences in successful rural development in the two cases. The sociopolitical constellations in Jibal Rayma and Anis formed different social foundations on which community development activities articulated through the LDAs were based. Anis was, in a sense, preadapted to meet the requirements for a well-functioning LDA; Jibal Rayma, with a very different sociopolitical organization, was not well adapted to meet the organizational and cooperative requirements of a successful development association.

CONTRIBUTIONS OF THE BOOK

This book is a problem-oriented ethnography. Apart from the specific questions addressing the problems of local development, it is also intended as a general ethnographic account of the western central highlands of Yemen. Anthropological study of Yemen only got underway in the mid-1970s; many gaps in the ethnographic coverage of Yemen remain. Because Yemen is undergoing rapid cultural change, most of the recent ethnographies have seized upon this as their dominant theme (Gerholm 1977; Tutwiler and Carapico 1981; Stevenson 1985). However, these studies have been concentrated either in the southern regions of the country or in the tribal regions north of the capital city Sana ͨa. Because this is one of the first studies set in the western central highlands located between the relatively well-studied Zaydi tribal areas in the north and the Shafi ͨi south, this research gives a view of Yemeni life that has not previously been documented.

As a situational study of indigenous development, this study may contribute toward an approach that takes more account of the complexities of the problems. The local and regional variations documented here may seem minor on the surface, but they often have important impact upon the success or failure of development projects. During the four years of this research, I had an opportunity to gain considerable personal experience with project planners and administrators. I noted a common tendency to ignore local diversity and variations in economics, history, political organization, and the like, in the development of project plans. The procedure most often followed was to develop a pilot project, often without knowledge of varying local conditions, and then to expand the project into other areas. The dubious assumption was that what was applicable in the small pilot area would be equally so elsewhere. Compounding the problem was the fact that most of these programs depended heavily on local organizations and contributions. This book shows that within Yemen there is considerable variation in local social organization and the ability to participate in development programs. By demonstrating the significance of local and regional variation, I hope that this study will have practical benefits for those intimately involved in rural development.

Finally, this book also addresses some theoretical issues in rural development, especially the role of traditional sociopolitical organizations in local development. The assertion that traditional social structures must undergo significant transformation before development can take hold has been made in the social science literature so often that it has become something of a bromide. Although social change is undoubtedly a basic element of development, there remains controversy over what kinds of changes must occur and whether or not traditional social systems are inevitably so dysfunctional as to impede development (Wiarda 1983:434).

Organization of the Book

The discussion is organized into two general sections. The first part sets the stage for the comparative analysis through a review of the general background of local development in Yemen. Chapter 2 presents the basic eco-cultural background of the areas and defines the units of comparison. Chapter 3 describes the general process and institutions involved in local development and documents differences in local development in two cases. The second part of this book constitutes the comparative analysis of local-level rural development. Chapter 4 identifies the common factors in the local development process and analyzes their influence on development. The remaining chapters explore the sociopolitical dynamics of local development in the western central highlands of Yemen.

2

Human Ecology

The western central highlands of Yemen are a land of considerable geographical contrast. The ecological zones range from humid tropical and arid desert regions to moderate mountain climates. As a part of the Red Sea and African Rift Valley fault systems, the western central region is predominantly mountainous country that rises abruptly from the flat Tihama coastal plain in the west to heights of over nine thousand feet before gradually tapering off toward the east and the great "empty quarter" (Rub^c al-Khali) desert. Three zones can be identified in this region, reflecting the main geographical, climatic, and cultural differences in the country.[1]

The Tihama is a flat coastal region averaging forty kilometers in width that forms the western perimeter of the western central highlands. The average yearly temperature of the Tihama is 86° (YARG 1982:30) with 70 percent relative humidity,[2] and the daily high in the summer regularly exceeds 100°. Although the Tihama is very humid, rainfall is less than 100 mm/year and agricultural land is eroded by high winds and shifting sands. The Tihama is crossed by numerous large wadi systems that drain the western Serat mountains and allow intensive cultivation on the floodplains and wadi bottoms. Spate irrigation predominates; but, due to a shallow water table, pump-fed agriculture is becoming much more common. Lying between the rich wadis are marginal semidesert and desert lands that can only support a few cactus and scrub bushes and are used for grazing camels and goats.

Rising sharply from the Tihama to the east of the Red Sea are the main mountain ranges of Yemen. The slope of the mountains is quite radical, often rising to over eight thousand feet within five or six kilometers. These rugged and relatively well watered slopes are intensively cultivated with a vast system of terraces built up and maintained over the centuries. Rainfall, most intense during the spring and summer maxima (April–June and July–September), is in the form of heavy tropical cloudbursts that typically form in mid-afternoon. The runoff is stored where possible in cisterns and small dams, but most cascades in torrents down steep watercourses into the wadi bottoms. A wadi may turn from a small stream into a rampaging river in the course of a few minutes, causing severe erosion and the destruction of crops in adjacent fields. The inability to harness the floodwaters means that, in spite of good rainfall, water is still often a problem for farmers. The mountain regions are not well forested due to frequent foraging for firewood and building timber and because most of the slopes are terraced for grain, coffee, and qat production.[3] The climate in the mountains is generally mild, only occasionally approaching freezing during the dry winter months. The third zone is the central plains and highland plateau. The plains are punctuated with valleys, tablelands, and volcanic cones and also receive moderately high rainfall, though somewhat less than the western mountain slopes. Most of the agriculture is rain-fed. The wide, richly cultivated fields near Yarim contrast with the northern plains around Saʿda, where the soils are barren and rocky and agriculture is limited. The climate in the plains is subject to greater extremes due to the lack of humidity from the Red Sea, and winter frost is common. The plains give way gradually in the east to the desert regions of the Rubʿ al-Khali, sparsely populated by a few Bedouin tribes.

Due to soil quality, rain shadows, and exposure, there are a variety of microenvironments within any zone. Thus, within the course of only a few kilometers, one may pass from verdant farmlands to areas that support only a few scrub plants and euphorbia. The steep terrain of much of the mountain region also accounts for dramatic climate changes within short distances.

AGRICULTURE: THE ECONOMIC BASE

Yemen has long been considered the garden spot of the Arabian Peninsula and is primarily a land of peasant farmers.[4] Not blessed with abundant mineral resources, but with adequate if variable rainfall, Yemen has traditionally had farming as an economic founda-

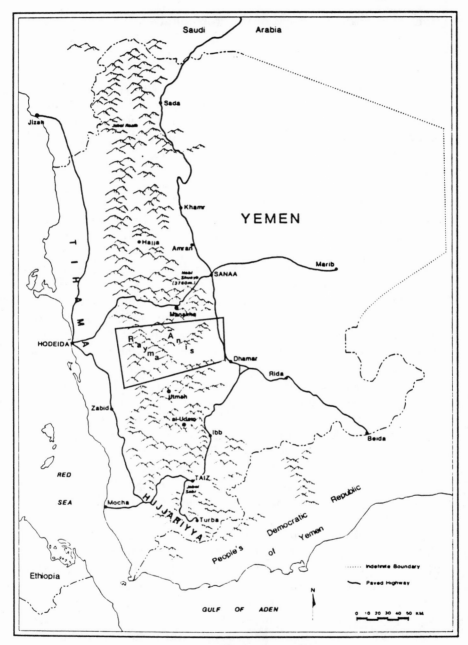

Map 1. Yemen Arab Republic

tion. More than 70 percent of the economically active population is directly engaged in agriculture (YARG 1983b:64), which accounts for anywhere from 35 to 70 percent of the gross domestic product, depending on the estimate.[5]

One of the most striking features of highland agriculture is the care and energy that have gone into the construction and maintenance of an extensive system of terraces that grace the mountain slopes: 49 percent of the cultivated land in Yemen is in terraced plots, while 51 percent lies in the plains area (Tihama and highland).

Agriculture is still labor-intensive. Tasks including plowing, sowing, leveling, fertilizing, removing crop residue, weeding and thinning, channeling the flow of irrigation waters, harvesting, and winnowing are all done primarily by hand. Most plowing is done with a single-blade plow drawn by oxen, donkeys, or camels, depending on the terrain. Some plowing is now done by tractor; but, given the mountainous environment, this is quite limited.

The basic unit in agricultural production is the extended family household. Within this unit, there is some division of labor. Men do the seasonal heavy work—such as plowing and repair of terraces— and the women the continuous work—weeding, thinning, and manure spreading. At harvest time, there is a high degree of cooperation, with every available hand helping out with the activities. The division of labor is more practical than absolute, and specialized roles are not very developed. One particular exception may be the custom of stripping the leaves from the maturing sorghum stalks. This procedure (*sharf*), which is said to concentrate all of the plant's energy into the formation of a large seed bulb, is carried out by the women. The job, although very difficult, is done in a happy atmosphere and accompanied by special work songs. Women do not work in the qat fields.

Crops and farming techniques vary in Yemen depending on the climate, topography, and, most importantly, availability of water supplies. Table 1 gives the breakdown of the relative percentages of the various crops grown in the region. The major crops in Yemen are the cereals, particularly sorghum, millet, corn, wheat, and barley. Most cereal production is for domestic consumption, and comparatively little is sold on the open market. Recently, the trend has been toward the production of food cash crops such as tomatoes, potatoes, and

Table 1. Percentage of Cultivated Land by Crop

cereals	88.4	fruits	0.6	vegetables	1.0
qat	4.4	sesame	0.4	other	1.6
legumes	1.8	tobacco	0.1		
cotton	1.6	dates	0.1		
Total	100.0				

Source: Revri 1983.

melons. Traditional cash crops were limited to coffee, cotton, tobacco, qat, and fruits (e.g., grapes, dates, papayas, mangoes, citrus).

Subsistence in the western central highlands is based on cereal farming supplemented by animal husbandry and cash cropping. As in other mountain regions of Yemen, the steep terrain has been made suitable for farming by terracing the steep slopes. These terraces are often not more than five or ten meters wide, prohibiting mechanization. Major crops include sorghum, wheat, barley, cowpea, and, recently, hybrid varieties of maize. The main cash crops suited to the region are qat and coffee. Each household may have one or two cows to provide dairy products and a number of chickens. The unfarmed marginal slopes are used for herding ruminants, mostly sheep and goats, which provide some animal protein in the largely cereal diet.

Water is the main limiting factor in agriculture, and various traditional methods have evolved to harness this valued resource. In the Tihama and wider wadis, earthen barrages are built or repaired on a yearly basis to control the torrential runoff from the mountains. Recently, bulldozers have simplified their construction and maintenance. Lands directly adjacent to the wadis are irrigated by systems of small rock dams built in the wadi itself. The back flow is directed into irrigation channels and onto the fields. This technique is well adapted to the environment because the dam is easy to construct and, in the event of a flood, is washed away, reducing the potential damage to the fields. The third traditional form, found mostly in the mountain areas, is to direct the flow of perennial springs into irrigation channels. A recent variation is to siphon water through long lengths of rubber hose. In the plains regions (including the Tihama), traditional lift systems were developed utilizing camels or

Table 2. Agricultural Schedule, Mountain Regions by Month

scheme 1.
```
  plow    plow and
  # # #   sow sorghum
  # # #     # # # #    harvest sorghum
  # # #     # # # #       # # #     sow barley/lentils
  # # #     # # # #       # # #       # #      harvest
  # # #     # # # #       # # #       # #           # #    plow
  # # #     # # # #       # # #       # #           # #   # #
O N D J F M A M J J A S O N D J F M A M J J A S O N D
```

Source: Dhamar Agriculture and Forestry Research Project.

donkeys to haul groundwater to the surface. The recent introduction of tube wells and pumps has replaced many of these.

Revri (1983:14) estimates that 62 percent of the cultivated land is rain-fed, 35 percent is spate-irrigated, and only 3 percent is irrigated through the use of pumps and other lift techniques. Only high-value cash crops like qat, coffee, and grapes and the small plots of alfalfa are irrigated regularly. The cereal crop is almost entirely rain-fed.

The rhythms of life in rural Yemen are defined in large part by the seasonal demands of agriculture. The time of most intensive activity begins in early spring when the fields are prepared for the planting of the year's sorghum harvest. Legumes are often planted with the sorghum as a symbiotic crop. Depending on the arrival of the spring rains, planting occurs between late March and early May (see table 2). The second intense period is the harvest peak, during the months of September and October. Wheat and barley are harvested and winnowed just prior to the sorghum. The actual harvest is done very rapidly; farmers work well into the night, laying the cut stalks in rows and separating the seed bulbs. The stalks are then bundled and stored for winter fodder. Every part of the plant is used. The period between August and November is completely dedicated to the year's agricultural production, with little time left for other activities.

The winter months are relatively free, except for repair and maintenance of the terraces and minor preparations on the fields. During this time and the few months of late spring and early summer, attention is focused on other activities, including building and local development projects.

Land Tenure

Sharecropping, with the usual division of 50 percent of the crop for the farmer and 50 percent for the landowner, is common. Actual arrangements may vary depending on the amount of input by the landowner. Although accurate data on land tenure are not readily available, results from a 1981 agricultural census carried out by the Ministry of Agriculture indicate that most farmers own some of their own land. About three-quarters of the agricultural areas are divided into holdings under ten hectares, and the average size of a holding is about one and a half hectares. The average family has one holding slightly over a hectare that is supplemented by contracting sharecropping agreements with large landowners.

Lands are classified according to ownership and title. Privately owned land (*milk*) is open to development and is regarded as personal property. Most of the agricultural land is of this variety. The custom of deeding land to the mosque either on a long-term lease or as an outright gift is also common. Such lands are designated as *waqf* properties under the administration of a representative of the Ministry of *Awaqf* (religious endowments). These lands are used to produce revenues for the maintenance of the local mosque and are sharecropped or farmed using volunteer labor from the community. Other types of lands are those owned by the state (*miri*) and the open tribal areas (*himi*, *fish*). These are usually undeveloped pasture and foraging lands. The state is the legal owner, but they are considered to be open lands and access is available to all residents of the area. According to informants, if an individual makes improvements on the open tribal land—for instance, constructing terraces—he may, through a process similar to homesteading, eventually acquire title to the lands. In actuality, most of the state and tribal lands are of such marginal agricultural potential that they are rarely, if ever, developed.

MARKETS

Traditionally, the western central highlands of Yemen supported a system of weekly markets (suqs). With the recent increase in rural road networks, they are being replaced by full-time shopkeeping.

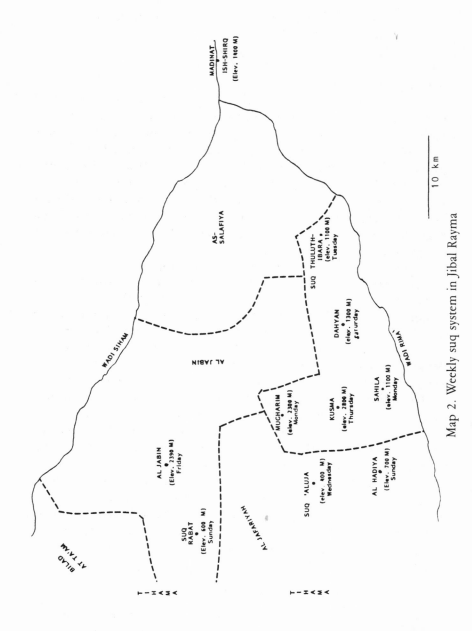

MADINAT
ISH-SHIRQ
(Elev. 1800 M)

AS-
SALAFIYA

WADI SIHAM

AL JABIN

SUQ THULUTH-
IBARA
(elev. 1100 M)
Tuesday

DAHYAN
(elev. 1300 M)
Saturday

WADI RIMÁ

MUGHARIM
(elev. 2300 M)
Monday

KUSMA
(elev. 2800 M)
Thursday

SAHILA
(elev. 1100 M)
Monday

AL JABIN
(Elev. 2390 M)
Friday

SUQ 'ALUJA
(elev. 400 M)
Wednesday

AL HADIYA
(Elev. 700 M)
Sunday

SUQ
RABAT
(Elev. 600 M)
Sunday

AL JAFARIYAH

BILAD
AT TA'AM

T-HAMA

T-HAMA

10 km

Map 2. Weekly suq system in Jibal Rayma

However, the institution of the weekly market is still an important feature in the more remote areas. The weekly suq system is regionally organized so that once each week market activity takes place in a central location. In the western central highlands, the distribution of markets in the Anis and Jibal Rayma regions is based on population density and travel time, so that a tribesman/farmer would have to journey no more than a couple of hours to reach the market and could easily conclude his transactions in one day. For example, the Jibal Rayma suq system includes both highland and lowland locations, depending on the day of the week. Map 2 shows the distribution of the weekly markets in this area. Main markets, such as Suq ᶜAluja and Kusma, are linked so that the lowland location (or terminal point of the road) is the wholesale depot for the highland retailers.

An example of a typical weekly suq is Kusma, Jibal Rayma. On most days of the week, the marketplace in Kusma is partially abandoned. Only a few dozen shops are open daily for business. Then, late Wednesday night and in the early hours of Thursday morning, the merchants who traveled the six- or seven-hour trail down the mountain to the Wednesday suq in ᶜAluja begin returning with their heavily burdened donkeys and preparing for the day's trade.

Early in the morning, the butchers slaughter and dress their animals while the permanent shop owners string brightly colored nylon and canvas covers between the shops and bring a large part of their inventory from the storerooms and set up temporary stalls. Itinerant vendors spread their wares out on the ground in the alleyways between the rows of shops.

By nine o'clock in the morning, the suq is in full swing. Something like a carnival atmosphere pervades; since it is considered forbidden to engage in any fight in the suq, tensions are at a minimum. The Kusma suq, on an average Thursday, swells to over five thousand people and well over one hundred merchants. In the same space where only three or four butchers work in the suq on a daily basis, fourteen or fifteen do business. Tables 3 and 4 give a breakdown of the shops and itinerant vendors on an average suq day. As in most Middle Eastern suqs (see Geertz 1979), shops selling similar items tend to be clustered together. By two o'clock in the afternoon, the main activity is over and the suq area returns to its semiabandoned atmosphere.

Table 3. Permanent Businesses in Kusma Suq, 1981

Grocer/dry goods	38	Electrical appliance	1
Repair (water pipes, etc.)	1	Tailor/clothing	10
Baskets	1	Storerooms	2
Butchers	6	Hardware	2
Cold store	1	Restaurant/tea shop	3
Hostel	3	Grain store	1
Blacksmith	6	Flour mill	2
		Qat	3

Total: 80

Table 4. Weekly Vendors in Kusma Suq, 1981

Grocery/dry goods	7	Fresh fruit	19
Tobacco	2	Cloth	2
Butcher	14	Grain	6
Spices/coffee	2	Popcorn	1
Leather goods	1	Charcoal	2
Ammunition	2	Audio cassettes, etc.	4
Greengrocers (*qushsham*)	9	Bread, milk (women)	7
		Qat	15

Total: 93

Note: Some weekly sellers are expansions of permanent businesses.

The highland tribesman now has a changing relationship with the suq. Traditionally, any close association with the marketplace was considered demeaning. However, with the increasing importance of a cash economy, more and more tribesmen are taking up trading in the suq as a livelihood. Now about one-third of the shopkeepers in Kusma are men who have always considered themselves tribesmen.

The suq is predominantly a male institution and it is still considered shameful for women of high social status to enter any crowded public place. The few lower-status women who are active in the suq, selling bread and precooked foods and baskets, are from market-based families. Tribal women who accompany their male relatives on suq day to help transport the purchases remain sitting together on the outskirts of the suq while the men do the shopping.

HUMAN GEOGRAPHY

Cultural diversity is very important when analyzing Yemen. The Tihama, with its hot and humid environment, has a distinctly African flavor. The most common type of house in rural areas is a round hut constructed of mud and wattle with a conical thatched roof. Most of the settlements in the Tihama are relatively large compounds encircled by fences of thorn and brush. Steffen et al. (1978) report that 79 percent of the settlements are greater than 250 inhabitants (i.e., more than 50 houses). The most densely populated regions of the Tihama are along the main wadi courses and in the slightly higher eastern regions adjacent to the mountains.

In the larger townships, rectangular houses made of baked clay brick with high ceilings are common. The main townships tend to be located along a north to south line in the center of the Tihama, equidistant from the mountains and the maritime communities and near the main wadi systems. These locations take advantage of the more moderate weather (less humidity) and facilitate trade with both the mountain and fishing/coastal communities.

The mountain areas are characterized by a much more dispersed settlement pattern. Multistory houses of rough-hewn stone typically line the ridges and rocky outcroppings. About two-thirds of all settlements are clusters of houses (*mahalat*) built wall-to-wall, with an average of ten houses per cluster.[6] Villages (*qura*) account for the remaining one-third of the settlements and typically are composed of thirty-five to forty-five households. Settlements much larger than these are rare in the mountain regions.

Moving into the plains region, settlements again become larger and more clearly defined, and freestanding households in the middle of agricultural fields are a rarity. People prefer to live in villages that have a fortresslike quality, typically containing a hundred or more houses. As in the mountains, houses tend to be multistory, but the mud-brick style of architecture is more common. To minimize the use of arable land for building, plains villages tend to be located on tablelike outcroppings or on the slopes of volcanic protrusions. Such a location provides for a commanding view of the fields while serving defensive purposes as well. The larger towns of Yarim, Dhamar, and Ma°bar, with populations between 6,000 and 20,000, as well as the major cities of Sana°a and Sa°da, are found in the plains regions.

As the plains decline into the arid regions of the Rub° al-Khali desert, villages are spaced farther apart and are generally limited to locations where there is adequate runoff for agriculture. The desert regions support a small Bedouin population who reside in tents and earn their livelihood primarily by goat herding.

In the western central highlands, there are very few settlements that could be called towns, and these are located only in the relatively flat plateau region. The majority of rural settlements are small housing clusters (*mahalat*) and villages (*qura*). To give a more concise picture of settlement patterns in Jibal Rayma and Anis, calculations on the percentage of villages and hamlets and their average size were made, based on 1981 census results (see table 5). Roughly two-thirds of the settlements are scattered hamlets of approximately ten houses built closely together, often sharing common walls, a cistern, and a small mosque. These settlements commonly are comprised of one large extended family unit with some shared economic ties. Although each household usually maintains its own economy, these closely related groups often engage in cooperation in time of peak agricultural labor demands and to make community improvements. This cooperation frequently consists of care and maintenance of the small mosque, cleaning the water cistern, and sharing the costs of expensive items such as an electric generator to supply power to the entire hamlet.

Highland villages (*qura*) are larger clusters of thirty to forty houses grouped in close proximity. A number of descent groups may be present, so there is less economic cooperation. The village typically has open public space for winnowing and threshing crops and a few small shops where dry and canned goods are sold, and the mosque is commonly *waqf* property. The line between a small village and a large hamlet is difficult to draw based on the number of houses, but is conceptually clear to its people.

The tradition of patrilocal residence common in Yemen is reflected in the tendency for houses to expand in size with each generation. A young couple often meets the need for more space in the family household by building an addition to the house. Therecent trend has been for young families to build new single-family dwellings,

Table 5. Settlement Patterns in the Western Central Highlands

Qada'	Settlement	N	%	Mean Household	Std. Dev.
Anis	villages	397	44.0	42.36	37.46
	hamlets	514	56.0	9.45	7.14
Total		911	100.0		
Jibal	villages	562	30.0	33.41	27.47
Rayma	hamlets	1,315	70.0	11.04	12.00
Total		1,877	100.0		

Note: Computed from 1981 CYDA census.

but new housing in the rural areas is still quite similar to the old in style.

In the older houses, the bottom floor (*sufala*) is used primarily for housing the domestic animals and storing winter fodder. The rooms are dark and the windows are small, allowing a minimum of ventilation. In prerevolutionary times, when intertribal feuding was more pronounced than it is today, houses were designed for defensive purposes so that the lower floors had little window space. Window space increases with the height of the building, and the largest room (*diwan*, *mufraj*) often has a commanding view. This room is set aside for socializing and family life and is generally quite colorful and spacious. The *mufraj* is the best-furnished room in the typical household, with cushions and bolsters lining the perimeter of the room. Carpets or crushed-cotton tapestries (often of the grand mosque in Mecca) are used to decorate the walls.

The typical highland house has few bedrooms, usually sparsely decorated. Larger houses may have a second *mufraj* reserved for the women when there is a large gathering of men. Kitchen facilities, which are used primarily for baking bread in the *tannur* oven, are usually located on the top floor or roof and are small, poorly lighted and ventilated, smoky, sooty work environments. Most food preparation is done outside on the rooftop or in the hallways, minimizing the time spent in the kitchen.

The walls of highland houses are at least two feet thick and are designed to maximize solar heating in the winter and shade cooling in the summer. Ideally, a house is oriented so that the sides with the

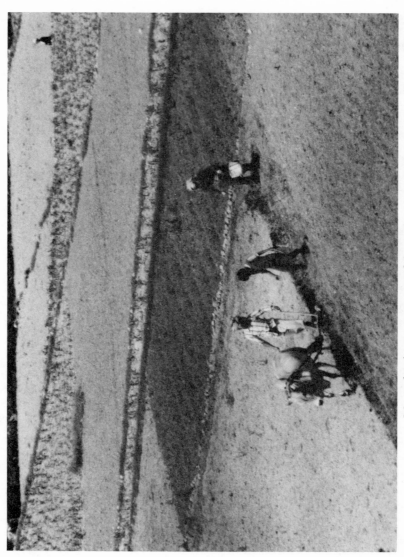

Man plowing, woman and boy planting seeds

Preparing terraces for spring planting

Highland Mahall, Jibal Rayma

Shaʿaf, Jibal Rayma

House of shaykh, Jibal Rayma

Village cluster, Jibal Rayma. High emigration community

Community-built school. Jibal Rayma

Kusma center, school (left foreground) and medical center (right foreground)

Modern housing

Dawran Anis health center

Highland women observing school pageant

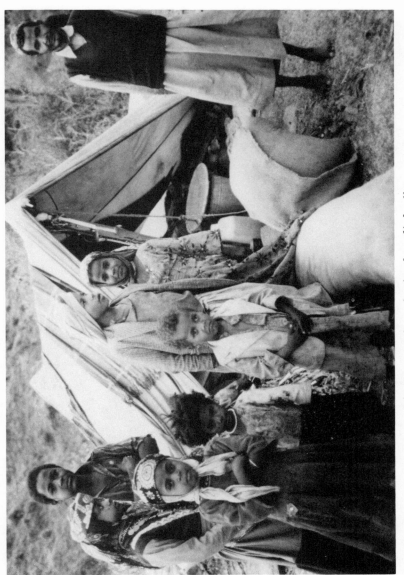

Itinerant workers, lowland wadi dwellers

Highland Plateau, Anis

Tihama housing

most window surface face south to absorb the winter sun, while the north-facing wall has little window space to promote cooling. The thickness of the walls serves to control the temperature of the house by slowly radiating the heat absorbed by the wall during the day into the house at night. The highland houses as well as their settlement patterns are well adapted to the environment.

3

Patterns of Rural Development

Since the 1962 revolution, Yemen has faced the monumental task of bringing an isolated agrarian-based society into alignment with the twentieth century. Toward this end, development projects, especially rural infrastructure building and improvements in the quality of life, have been undertaken and financed largely through local initiative. This chapter reviews the kinds of development activities that are of primary importance in the western central highlands in light of the various barriers to economic development and other socioeconomic factors. While the overall economic situation in rural Yemen is conducive to local development, it is interesting to note that little has been done to improve the traditional economic base of the rural regions, especially grain production. Instead, as we shall see, peasant farmers in the western central highlands have opted for alternative investment and development strategies that emphasize improving the immediate quality of life and have concentrated on basic infrastructure building.

PUBLIC AND PRIVATE DEVELOPMENT

It is important to draw a distinction between new investments, construction, improvements, and other development activities that are in the public sector, and those that are essentially private enterprise. Both are significant in the overall changing picture of rural life, but they are based on different financial resources and involve different forms of social organization. In the private sector, development in the western central highlands typically includes activities such as home improvement, electrification, new businesses and trade, and, to some extent, agricultural improvements and investments. In the public

45

sector, clinics, schools, community water supplies, roads, and the like constitute the main activities. Private development is mostly concerned with direct economic activities and improving the quality of life within the household unit, while public development is mostly concerned with infrastructure and services.

Economic Change and Private Development

The private development (indeed, development in general) that is occurring throughout Yemen is directly related to the profound economic changes that have taken place in the past twenty years. To understand the form that development has taken in the rural regions, it is important to view it within the changing economic context.

One of the basic economic arguments posited by modernization theorists to explain economic stagnation in peasant societies like Yemen is that a vicious circle of low income and inadequate savings inhibits investments that may increase production (Singer 1949; Nurkse 1953; Hagen 1962; Cooper 1972; Foster 1973). This argument reasons that since peasant societies engage in agriculture at a near-subsistence level, the farming household must consume almost everything it produces. The limited surpluses that are available for sale on the market produce only enough revenue to purchase items such as tools, clothing, food staples, fuels, medicines, and the like that are necessary for its maintenance. In this economic situation, there is little opportunity for the peasant to amass significant savings for investment and expansion. Such a no-growth condition provides little in the way of surplus that could be transformed into community improvements.

This scenario was typical of Yemen until the revolution, but since then the economic picture has changed so radically as to make the lack of savings argument highly questionable. The farmer in the western central highlands still operates at just above subsistence level, especially where grain production is concerned, but other sources of income have emerged to break the cycle of low income and inadequate savings. Many theorists on rural development discount the effects of cash injected into traditional economies from outside sources, through expatriate remittances, because historically these amounts have been relatively low. But the situation in Yemen is atypical of most developing countries, requiring a reassessment of the importance of remitted income for development.

One of the ramifications of the 1962 revolution was an end of the isolationist policies of the imams, allowing among other things a much higher rate of emigration. By the mid-1970s, an estimated 40 percent of the male population was employed outside of Yemen (Cohen and Lewis 1979b:1). Particularly attractive were the opportunities in neighboring Saudi Arabia and the Gulf states. Prior to the 1960s, most of the emigration from the imamic regime was from the southern regions. East Africa, Sudan, and the United States were the most popular destinations. The situation changed dramatically in the 1970s when the rapid influx of petro-dollars into the Saudi and Gulf economies stimulated intensive growth and the demand for workers in those countries. Yemen became valued as a source of labor in construction and in the service sector. This new demand, coupled with the lure of high wages, stimulated increased emigration from other regions of Yemen, including the western central highlands.

In addition to external emigration, expanded business opportunities in the urban areas as a result of the "open door" free trade policies of the republican government, foreign investments in businesses, grants-in-aid to the government sector, and, to some extent, development projects themselves have stimulated increased rural to urban migration. In the government services sector, compensation to employees jumped from 250 million rials (4.54 rials equal $1 U.S.) in 1972 to 2,454 million rials in 1982 (YARG 1983b:337), indicative of a dramatic increase in employment opportunities and salaries.

Since the end of the civil war, Yemen's economy has become further linked to the economies of Saudi Arabia and the Gulf states, marking its increased dependence on what Wallerstein (1974) has termed the world capitalist system. The ramifications can be seen from the national to the household level. Almost every household has at least one member who is actively engaged in some kind of wage-earning occupation, whether as a migrant worker, a tradesman, or in the rapidly expanding military and government services sectors. A profound shift has occurred, placing new emphasis on cash in what was recently a near-subsistence-level agriculture economy.

One of the major consequences of emigration and increased wage-earning employment has been the development of what has been termed a capital surplus, labor-short situation in the rural areas (Cohen

and Lewis 1979b:3).[1] An examination of some economic indicators—
including higher wages, inflation, increased consumer spending and
patterns of savings, along with changes in the national accounts of
Yemen—supports the argument that more than adequate local
resources, particularly liquid assets, exist to support development activities.

Wages

Increases in local wages are one good indication of a cash surplus
in the rural areas. Although farming is still the main occupation, it
only requires intensive labor by the male population for part of the
year. Most men also supplement their earnings through casual employment in the local construction industry, trading, shopkeeping, or
personal services. Swanson reports that wages in the southern regions
escalated dramatically in the 1970s. An unskilled laborer's daily wage
jumped from 5 rials in 1974 to 60 rials in 1977 (Swanson 1979:17).
During my research in the western central highlands, the spiraling
inflation continued as the daily wage for an unskilled worker rose
from 50 rials per day in 1980 to 80 per day in 1983. Similarly, the
cost of skilled laborers such as stonemasons and jackhammer operators (for blasting building stone) jumped from 350 rials per day in
1980 to 500 rials per day in 1983. A young local leader who often
was called upon to mediate minor disputes reported earning over
6,000 rials in one month (Ramadan 1982), while a local *sahi* (nurse)
typically received 500 rials for an afternoon house call and two vita-
min injections. Soldiers received between 100 and 200 rials for respond-
ing to a request for police services; and even the *dawshan* (crier) at
weddings received from 200 to 300 rials for his services. It is clearly
no exaggeration to say that, across the board, wages and savings have
skyrocketed in the rural areas.

Inflation

A recent indication of a cash surplus in the local economy can be
seen in the general inflation of prices of all domestically produced
(*baladi*) and culturally valued items. A few examples may illustrate.
Grapes, which have remained constant in supply over the years, rose
from 2 rials per kilogram in 1974 to over 20 rials per kilogram in
1982. A sheep, which in the mid-1970s was valued at around 50
rials, sold for over 400 rials in 1983. Locally grown sorghum increased

in price from an already-inflated 1978 price of 51 rials per sack (*qada*) to 75 rials in 1982. The biggest jumps can be seen in land and building costs and in bride prices. Swanson reports that land values in Taᶜiz between 1974 and 1976 multiplied by at least ten; prime irrigated farm land jumped in price from around $3,500 to over $70,000 per acre between the early 1960s and 1976 (1979:71, 82); the same increases are found in the western central highlands.

The costs of establishing a household have also escalated. Bride prices, although theoretically limited to 15,000 rials by President al-Hamdi, averaged 80,000 YR in 1984. In contrast, in the early 1970s, a man could secure a bride for around 3,000 YR. In 1975, a rural school with six classrooms and second-story office space was built in Kusma for under 40,000 YR. In 1981, the cost of an addition to a house (one large room, a small, unfinished bathroom, and a storage room) barely a hundred meters from the school cost 250,000 YR.

Consumerism

Another indicator of an increased amount of cash in the western central highlands is the dramatic rise in consumer items previously unobtainable. Even in Kusma, Jibal Rayma, one of the most isolated areas in all of Yemen, 40 to 50 percent of the households have television sets. Small black-and-white models, initially used in the area, were quickly put aside in favor of color models well before their use-life was over. Video cassette recorders soon followed, and, of course, the portable audio cassette radio-recorder is ubiquitous. The availability of television spurred a rapid movement toward rural electrification. In Jibal Rayma prior to late 1979, there was little need for electricity and only a few houses in all the region had power. Lighting was provided by kerosene lanterns. With the arrival of color television came a new demand for electricity; in the course of one year, over 50 percent of the houses in this isolated rural area were electrified by portable generators. Colored fluorescent lamps were commonly set on the rooftops merely for decorative purposes. Other electrical appliances, including hot plates, blenders, and battery chargers, soon began appearing in a few houses but were not as widespread because of their limited utility.

The recent accumulation of garbage is also indicative of increased consumerism. Prior to the 1970s, almost all waste was organic and was usually devoured by semidomestic dogs, so accumulation of trash

was not a problem; there was no system for its disposal in rural settlements. Trash accumulation of plastic wrappers, aluminum cans,
plastic shoes, thermos bottles, junk parts from broken-down cars,
and all matter of waste associated with packaged goods has now become
endemic. In some rural suqs, the trails leading into the market are
literally paved with crushed Pepsi Cola cans—unsavory proof of economic change and increased money in the rural communities.

Qat
    A final example indicative of increased cash surplus in the rural
economy is the significant increase in production and consumption
of qat (Varisco 1986:6). A mild stimulant, qat has been chewed for
centuries in Yemen. It is usually chewed for four or five hours in
social settings that are quite ritualized (Gerholm 1977:176–85;
Kennedy et al. 1980; Kennedy 1987). Although qat use has been a
custom in Yemen for probably over five hundred years, prior to the
late 1960s and early 1970s its production and consumption were on
a more limited scale. Ameen Rihani (1930) remarks that qat was the
daily custom of the soldiers in the imam's army and among the civil
servants. Qat is now becoming a daily experience for most people in
the producing areas, and its use is increasing throughout the country. Qat prices vary from region to region and according to its quality. In 1982, the average price for a bundle (*zurba*, *rubta*) of average
quality qat in Jibal Rayma was 30 rials. Lesser-quality qat such as
sawti and *harami*, mostly consumed by the lower-income classes, sold
for around 10 rials.
    For the majority of people who chew qat on a regular basis, it
can be an expensive pastime. A young leader in Kusma estimated
that his monthly salary of 2,000 YR from the Ministry of Education
as director of schools for the district (a part-time occupation) would
not cover his monthly qat expenses.[2] In short, the enormous amount
of money spent on qat is another indicator of the capital surplus in
rural Yemen.

Savings Patterns and National Accounts
    Some inferences can also be drawn from examples of patterns of
household savings and a review of national financial accounts. Unfortunately, at the household level, it is difficult to get a clear idea of
how much actually exists in the form of cash savings. In the rural

areas, it is customary to keep large sums of cash locked away in strongboxes inside the house; rural families make little use of the central banking system.[3] On occasion, I was able to witness business transactions, so a few typical examples may demonstrate the trend. One farmer who had a small plot of qat (less than one-third hectare) and occasionally worked in Saudi Arabia had in excess of 40,000 YR cash in his strongbox. In another case, a relatively unimportant shaykh kept over 100,000 YR cash on hand for his farming and household operating expenses. It is difficult actually to document just how generalized savings are, but the general sense gained by living among the rural farmers over four years was that there were ample opportunities to accrue savings and that it was a common practice.

Given the greater costs of construction and weddings, if savings were not possible, one would not expect increased construction activities and wedding parties would be fewer and more low-key. In Kusma, an isolated community with eighty six houses, nine new houses were constructed between 1980 and 1982, three major additions were made, and around a dozen major improvements (converting roofs, caulking sides) were completed. According to informants, weddings, major affairs that usually lasted three days, continued at about the same rate as always. The main difference is that now they have an astronomic cost (over 50,000 YR for the party itself)![4]

Finally, a look at national money supply figures indicates dramatic increases over the past few years (see table 6).[5] Between 1973 and 1981, the money supply increased over thirteenfold, a powerful indicator of the new influx of cash into the Yemen economy.

This description of economic indicators sheds some light on the problem of assessing the economic situation in the rural areas. The evidence certainly indicates that there are sufficient amounts of cash in the rural areas to finance some development activities. In the western central highlands, as in other regions of Yemen, the increased importance of cash and wage labor has broken the cycle of low earnings and inadequate savings that rural economists have theorized as a basic barrier to development.

Inadequate Markets

Another common argument posited as a barrier to development that has particular significance in the western central highlands is the "vicious circle of inadequate markets" (Hagen 1962:42). In undevel-

Table 6. Yemen Arab Republic, Money Supply by Year

1973	1975	1977	1979	1981
728.3	2509.1	6205.1	8822.6	9905.2

Source: YARG 1981:226; YARG 1983b:193.
Note: In millions of rials: $1 U.S. equals 4.54 Yemeni rials (YR).

oped countries, the lack of adequate markets for surpluses naturally mitigates against increasing production. In highland Yemen, this situation holds true for a number of reasons: (1) historically, there has not been a large, well-structured market for selling surplus grains; (2) competition from imported grains has made local production for the market noncompetitive; and (3) recent trends in consumer preferences in the urban areas have lessened the demand for locally produced grains.

Most of the grain produced in Yemen was for immediate consumption (Steffen et al. 1978:14). Surpluses were only produced by larger landowners who marketed their production through an agent or middleman (*wakil*); there has never been a close direct relationship between grain producers and the sellers in the market. Furthermore, it was traditionally considered dishonorable for tribesmen, the main producers of cereals, to have close dealings with the suq (Gerholm 1977). Surpluses were limited, as was the number of grain agents, and a large marketing system was not developed. Dostal, Serjeant, and Wilson (1983:274) report in their analysis of highland markets that grain accounted for only 4.34 percent of the goods for sale in the major suq, and personal observations in Jibal Rayma and Anis also indicate that cereals were not a major marketed commodity. In Kusma suq, a large regional market, only one merchant dealt in local grains, and little grain was seen for sale in the main market towns of Isla[c], Hadiqa, and Madinat ish-Shirq in Anis. The cultivation of cereals is still mainly production for the household. Cereals are primarily circulated at the level of exchange between groups of relatives and between the households of a settlement (Dostal, Serjeant, and Wilson 1983:274).

Of course, the nonfarming segment of society and urban residents were historically dependent on locally produced grain, but the bulk of these supplies were obtained from *waqf* (religious endowment) lands that sold the production on the market and from the government-owned grain stores that sold supplies collected as *zakat* tax. *Zakat* on grain was assessed at 10 percent for rain-fed fields and 5 percent for irrigated lands.

Despite recent studies of social stratification (Gerholm 1977; Stevenson 1981) that demonstrate that the tribesman's traditional aversion to earning a living in the market is weakening (it is now less "shameful" to market produce directly in the suq), there has not been a significant increase in marketing cereals. Locally produced grain is now no longer competitive with imported supplies. In an economy with a situation of capital surplus accompanied by a labor shortage, wages for occasional labor have become inflated, driving up the production costs of domestic grains and encouraging a shift to other crops.

Table 7 presents a comparison of wholesale and retail prices for locally produced (*baladi*) cereals and imported wheat, showing a consistent pattern in which imported wheat is priced significantly lower than locally produced cereals. Swanson reports an increase of 300 percent in the early 1970s (1979:77), and Steffen et al. report (1978) an increase in expenditures for imported cereals, from 3 million rials in 1964 to 325 million rials in 1975–76 (1978:27). This trend has continued into the 1980s.

Data on the national production of cereals, depending on the source, indicate that it has either remained stable or declined, but it has definitely not increased. In his study of three villages in the southern part of the country, Swanson (1979) also reports a steady decline in cereal production. Statistical yearbook reports, which are aggregated for all Yemen and are admittedly somewhat unreliable due to a lack of agricultural census data, show a constant level of production with the exception of 1975, when there was an abundant rainfall. The most recent Yemen government assessments of the agricultural production in Yemen show a decline in grain production of 14 percent between 1975–76 and 1981–82. However, these statistics do not adequately reflect the degree of the decline in highland production because they are offset by the increases resulting from pump irrigation and mechanization in the Tihama. Dostal, Serjeant, and Wilson report that in the Tihama grains make up 37.50 percent of the weekly market, whereas in the highlands they make up only 3.23

Table 7. Comparative Grain Prices in Dhamar Suq

	Wholesale prices per qada			
	1979	1980	1981	1982
Imported wheat	.67	.70	.62	.67
Local wheat	.97	1.19	1.20	1.36
Local sorghum (white)	.70	.81	.99	.74
Local sorghum (red)	.56	.65	.64	.53
	Retail prices per kilogram			
		1980	1981	1982
Imported wheat		2.19	2.13	2.15
Local sorghum (red)		3.00	2.50	2.04
Local sorghum (white)		3.00	2.75	2.87

Source: YARG 1983*b*.
Note: The *qada* is a volume measure roughly equivalent to a large gunnysack. Of course, a *qada* of wheat weighs more than a *qada* of sorghum. No prices are published for local wheat, reflecting its low volume on the market.

percent (1983:273), further indicating that the Tihama region produces a higher surplus of grains. In the highland regions, there is little question that cereal production is on the decline; the ever-increasing numbers of abandoned terraces are vivid testimony to this fact.

Another factor in the decline of grain production in the highlands that should be taken into consideration may be the reduced demand in the urban areas for local grains. Part of this is attributable to changing consumer tastes. The traditional breads in the cities made from sorghum or local wheat or barley are rapidly being replaced by the white loaves (*ruti*) and pocket breads (*shami*) produced in commercial bakeries that use processed imported white flour. These breads are particularly popular in the ever-increasing number of small restaurants that serve a more Westernized menu. Also, the white breads are increasingly common in urban households (Adra 1982). The unfavorable market conditions, competition from cheaper imports, and changing patterns of consumer demand work to make production of cereals for market consumption unattractive.

Ecological Limitations

A final barrier to the development of cereal farming that must be evaluated is the basic ecological limitation existing in the highland regions. As mentioned earlier, most grain production is based on dry-farming techniques. Located on the northern fringes of the East Africa/Indian Ocean monsoon system, Yemen is subject to yearly variations in rainfall and occasional extended periods of drought (Steffen et al. 1978:26). This makes cereal production a tenuous occupation at best. Water resources that are sufficient for large-scale irrigation are extremely limited in the highland regions, and their exploitation can be too expensive for the average farmer to consider. For example, in the high plateau region of Anis near Ma^{c}bar, the water table is more than 100 meters deep. Drilling a tube well through layers of basalt in 1983 cost in excess of 500,000 rials, well beyond the means of all but the wealthiest landowners. The high evaporation rates and heavy sediment loads of the runoff make large storage dams unfeasible, limiting the possibilities for efficient storage and use of surface waters. Furthermore, the steep mountainous terrain of the western central highlands has only allowed the construction of narrow rural roads, making access to potential well sites by large drilling rigs all but impossible. Increasing grain production through irrigation in the western central highlands is not a realistic alternative because of the basic limits of exploitable water resources.

In addition, the nature of the terrain in highland Yemen has made mechanization impossible in all but the plains regions. In the more level sections of the western central highlands, only a small amount of new land has been brought under mechanized cultivation. The use of bulldozers to build dikes in land adjacent to watercourses that otherwise would be subject to seasonal flooding has been the one notable exception in the region, but these improvements have been confined to wadi bottomlands and are limited in number. Examination of aerial photographs of the Ma^{c}bar/Jahran plains in Anis taken in 1973, before the tractor was in common use (in 1973 only sixty three tractors were imported into the country; YARG 1977:77), indicates that little new land has been placed under cultivation. Instead, the major benefit of that mechanization has been the maintenance of previous production levels, particularly in light of the labor shortages resulting from emigration.

PATTERNS OF PRIVATE INVESTMENT

Despite the fact that cereal farming has traditionally been the backbone of the rural economy, it is quite evident that development geared to increasing production has not been an important focus of the highland Yemeni farmer (Ross 1981:7; Steffen et al. 1978:26; Cohen and Lewis 1979b:14; Swanson 1979). In the western central highlands, the marginally productive terraces that were formerly cultivated in grain have been abandoned. As an example, in Wadi as-Sayyid, Jibal Rayma, over 500 terraces on the lowest slopes of Jabal Huzar and Jabal Dhulumlum are beyond repair. A resident from the nearby village of Hadiya cited difficult access, marginal rainfall, and lack of interest as reasons for their abandonment. This disinterest is due to a growing preference among farmers for wage employment, which allows them to buy cheap imported grain rather than farm the distant slopes for at best marginal returns.

A similar pattern existed in Anis; sometimes even minor investments, which could have brought extensive tracts back into use, were not made. For example, in community of Maghrabit al-ᶜAnis (ᶜuzla in Jabal ish-Shirq nahiya), an entire hillside of terraces below the ruins of an ancient village has been abandoned and left to decay. These terraces, estimated to cover about five hectares, are in excellent condition given the fact that they have been abandoned for a few years. They are located just to the north and below the level of a good-quality perennial spring that provides drinking water for the hamlets and waters the mosque's waqf lands. Most of the spring water is left to run off the mountainside, where it disappears quickly into the wadi alluvium below. A minor investment of a couple of hundred meters of rubber hose could easily irrigate these abandoned terraces with the unutilized runoff, yet no one has considered the investment worthwhile (the climate is not appropriate for growing qat). Even in the quality lands, there has been little investment in techniques to increase grain production.

Cash Cropping and Qat Production

Simply to state that little agricultural investment is occurring in the western central highlands is misleading without discussing alternatives that have developed. Agriculture is the only realistic land use of the rural areas, and there has been a movement toward increasing

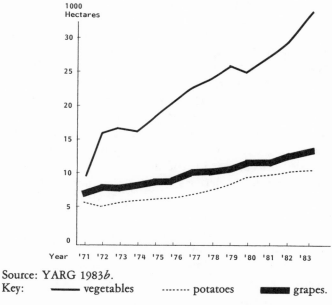

Source: YARG 1983*b*.
Key: ────── vegetables ········ potatoes ▰▰▰ grapes.

Figure 1. Area in production of selected cash crops

production of cash crops. In areas accessible by four-wheel-drive vehicles and with adequate water supplies, crops with direct marketability, such as vegetables like tomatoes, potatoes, onions, and melons, have been popular alternatives. For example, potato production has increased by 72.4 percent, vegetable production by 42.6 percent, and fruit production by 34.6 percent over the latter half of the 1970s (YARG 1982:7). Figure 1 shows the trend in increasing acreage in these kinds of crops. Also, citrus production has been successful in the warmer, well-watered wadi regions near Hammam ʿAli. However, by far the most common alternative has been to invest in qat production.

Qat has been the most popular choice for a number of reasons. First, because it is a hardy plant and fairly resistant to drought, there is little risk involved in its cultivation. Even in the event of unforeseen frost damage, the small leaves can be harvested and sold as a variety known as *zabib*. Second, a vast marketing network exists for qat, and even the most remote areas such as Kusma in Jibal Rayma have efficient means for sale and transport. For example, enough qat can be carried on the back of a porter from the fields to the regional market to earn him an average of 100 YR per trip. In areas accessible by motor vehicle, much larger quantities of qat are handled by whole-sale agents (*wakala'*) and are then resold to the individual dealers (*maqawwitin*). For all involved in the qat trade, the profits are quite high. For example, one *wakil* in the qat market in al-Qa^c, Sana^ca, reported earning 30,000 rials in one month.

The demand for qat is consistently high; although seasonal vari-ations allow for some price fluctuation due to supply, qat is always a profitable commodity. In comparing the economics of qat produc-tion with all other agricultural activities, Revri concludes that "the gross margin per hectare of qat in comparison with all other crops is at least tenfold" (1983:84). Consequently, in areas where it can be grown, much of the private investment in the agricultural sector has gone into qat production. In areas with limited water resources, small water projects have been used for domestic supplies and irrigation of cash crops, especially qat.

Nonagricultural Investments

A few cases drawn from Kusma, Jibal Rayma, may best illustrate the patterns of other investment typical in the rural areas.

Three brothers, ^cAbd al-Rahman, Samir, and Hussayn, had spent the past nine years working in Saudi Arabia for an American con-struction firm. When they returned, each chose a different strategy for investing what funds, if any, they had saved. ^cAbd al-Rahman, a man of marginal character who was the oldest of the brothers and known as a clown and therefore not taken seriously by the commu-nity, returned home with no savings at all. His brothers reported that he had frittered away all of his earnings while in Saudi Arabia.

Samir, on the other hand, had purchased a number of items that he felt would set him up in a business in Kusma. He returned with a 3½-kilowatt diesel generator, battery charger, electric iron, washing machine, and a variety of tools and electronic gadgets. He rented a shop just outside his family home, about fifty meters from the main suq, and set up shop. Until then, there had been few gen-erators in Kusma; since television had just recently reached the area, people were using automobile storage batteries to run the televisions. Of course, they needed periodic recharging, which was done for 40 rials apiece. Given that there were about thirty televisions in the dis-trict center at the time, Samir felt that he would soon recoup his investment and turn a profit. Unfortunately, many other returning workers had also purchased generators; in the course of six months, the entire settlement was electrified and his battery-charging business was soon obsolete. However, his shop was diversified. He ran a laundry business with his washing machine and iron and made a little money at that. In addition, he used a blender to make fruit juices, which he sold during suq day. He also had a watch repair and electric repair business. Initially, he reported making 7,000 rials a month; but soon his business began to falter, and the only viable investment left was selling surplus power from his generator to other households, at 30 rials a month per light bulb (neon, 20 watt). This barely covered his fuel and transportation expenses; so, after about eight months, he gave up on that business. He still had some savings and did odd jobs around the community fixing generators; about a year and a half later, when the roadway reached a flat area named Magharam, two hours' walk from Kusma, he set up a restaurant that did a reasonable business.

Hussayn put his savings into the construction of a new house in a nearby hamlet, completing the four rooms of the bottom floor (at a cost of around 200,000 rials). Samir and Hussayn also financed cementing the roof of their father's home.

A few other cases may further illustrate.

Ghalib was not very educated, but his menial job in Saudi Arabia afforded him the ability to save around 50,000 rials. When he returned, he joined in a partnership with another man from the market. His partner was a very intense, hardworking, middle-aged man who was the father of three sons and owned a hotel, tea shop, and cold store (freezer with frozen chickens powered by his own generator). Together, they expanded the business, added a second story to the hotel, and refurbished the restaurant, adding new tables and repainting, as well as rebuilding the inside with a cement floor, mirrors, and a glass door. Ghalib ran the restaurant, while the sons of the co-owner worked as waiters and busboys. Restaurant patrons are notorious for shouting curses and obscenities at the waiters and cooks, dropping food on the floors, and general messiness. The chaos of the restaurant soon took its toll. After about five months, Ghalib gave up his share in the partnership and returned to Saudi Arabia, where he felt that he was much happier. He never was able to marry.

Hassan was a young man in his early twenties. He spent six years in Saudi Arabia working as a salesperson in the perfume section of a department store. When he returned to his hamlet, about an hour's walk from Kusma, he moved back into his father's home. He purchased a number of household niceties — rugs, carpets, television, brass fixtures, and electric supplies to wire his home. He also was part-owner of a new diesel generator (the average price for a generator was 10,000 rials). But his biggest investment was to take a wife. The total cost of the wedding party and bride price (*shart*) came to about 135,000 rials! After his wedding, he set up shop as a perfume and electrical supplies dealer in Suq ʿAluja. His very small business met with limited success.

As these cases suggest, the most popular nonagricultural alternative for many returned migrants has been to invest in small businesses, particularly retailing and small trade. The increase in imports over the last decade has created new opportunities for small businesses in rural areas, and villages and hamlets that were once entirely dependent on the weekly suqs now contain a number of small general merchandise shops. Cold stores have been popular investments and are invariably stocked with imported frozen chickens. Other varieties of new businesses, particularly in the regional markets, include electrical repair, building supplies and lumber, restaurants, jewelry and appliance shops, ready-made clothing stores, and automobile repair shops (tire repair, body shops, mechanics, gas stations, etc.). As mentioned earlier, the stigma attached to maintaining a business in the suq has lessened considerably since emigration has become widespread. Recently, many tribal farmers have supplemented their livelihood by investing in businesses in the marketplace. Only a few large-scale businesses have appeared in the rural areas, most notably chicken-breeding farms operated under a franchise with a national corporation.

Construction is another form of investment that has been booming in many areas of the western central highlands. The Yemen statistical yearbook indicates that for the country as a whole there was growth in the construction sector from 134 million rials in 1970 to 2,863 million rials in 1980! Construction, of either homes or businesses, is one of the few risk-free avenues of investment and therefore has been the most common choice among the limited set of possible alternatives. Along with the construction of new homes, improvements on older buildings—caulking the outside stone walls with cement, cementing or whitewashing the traditional dirt roofs, installing rudimentary indoor plumbing, and electrification—are common. One result of the construction boom has been the expansion of the hardware and building supply retail sector.

The growth of the rural road networks has greatly increased the opportunities for business associated with transport and equipment maintenance. One very common practice is to purchase a Toyota station wagon and open a rural taxi service. This part of the transportation system, which was once completely free-lance, is now state-regulated, and all taxis must be licensed to operate. My rough estimate is that in 1982 there were about 50 taxis in Jibal Rayma (where there are limited roads), and over 500 in Anis. In Dhamar governorate, 1,204 taxis were registered between 1978 and 1982 (YARG 1983*b*:119).

A few individuals have also invested in heavy machinery, especially bulldozers and tractors, which are contracted out by the day to farmers; given the high investment costs, this is still a very limited practice. Throughout the countryside where roads are completed, small businesses have been set up for automotive and equipment maintenance. An interesting feature is the extent to which these services are segregated. At a gas station it is not possible to buy motor oil, which is sold in a separate shop usually located near the station. Tire repair is also available only at another independent business. The same holds for garage mechanics, lubrication stations, and the like.

In the western central highlands, there is little variation in these patterns. Private investment has been even across the region. The most notable exception is in the transportation sector, more developed in Anis, where there is a better system of rural roads, than in Jibal Rayma, where roads are limited. Otherwise, the rate of construction, the pattern of establishing new shops and businesses, and the trend of shifting from grain to cash crops are constant across this region.

PUBLIC-SPONSORED DEVELOPMENT

Development activities in the public domain are principally of three types: community-sponsored projects that are financed by local contributions or informal taxation; projects that are undertaken by the local development associations (*ta^c awaniyat*) that utilize a combination of local contributions, public funds, and government cost sharing; and projects sponsored by the central government and its agencies, which include foreign development aid. Given the varieties of public-sponsored development, it is important to distinguish between development that is the result of local initiative — that is, development from below — and that which is delivered through the state administrative system's hierarchy — or development from above.

The programs underway in the western central highlands are aimed at improving and introducing innovations in agricultural and livestock production, health care services, education and vocational training, road building and public works projects, and rural electrification. These projects reflect the government-set priorities for rural development and are the major efforts at development from above. Many have a large input from foreign donor agencies, and all are implemented through the appropriate ministries.

Improved health service is one of the major development activities in Yemen. The Ministry of Health has partially financed health centers, provided stipends and supplies to rural health posts, and sponsored immunization malaria-control programs. Unfortunately, change in the rural areas is a slow process, and these projects have met with limited success, achieving only partial coverage in the rural areas. There is a significant contribution in this field from outside sources, and a number of rural health centers and health development programs have been financed through bilateral aid agreements with Western governments and neighboring Arab countries.

Primary schools in the rural areas have been partially financed by the Ministry of Education and are rapidly increasing in number. To counter the shortage of trained Yemeni teachers, the majority of the teaching positions are filled by Egyptian and Sudanese teachers who work in Yemen on five-year contracts. It is very common to find teachers assigned to areas with no official school facilities teaching in temporary buildings.

Agricultural extension offices are limited to the larger towns and their services confined to areas included in the rural road network. Their main activities include distributing information on seed types, fertilizing schedules, and insecticide use. A few agricultural research stations are situated in the highlands plains and are part of international development efforts.

Local Initiative Development : The LDAs

The second major type of public-sponsored development is under-taken through the local development associations. The limited resources of the central government, combined with the need to improve the standard of living in the rural areas, resulted in the formation of locally based development associations. The strategy that evolved in Yemen incorporated many features frequently associated with development from below. The Yemen model incorporated a rural-based development strategy with a community or regional focus that utilized locally generated resources.

Customs of community-level cooperation have been a traditional feature of western central highlands society; prior to the revolution and subsequent economic boom, most public works such as improved mountain trails were maintained through organized cooperative projects supported and financed by the families of the villages. Tribes and tribal groups have always been strongly independent, managing their affairs without significant input from the centralized power structures, and this tradition continued, taking a new form in the local development associations.

The cooperative movement's beginnings trace back to the period just after the 1962 revolution. The movement arose with the realization that the new republican central government was faced with the primary task of state building and was too weak to undertake rural development. The cooperatives resulted "from popular demand for better infrastructures and social services, the inability of the central government to provide these, and the increased flow of financial resources due to remittances from emigration to Saudi Arabia and the Gulf states" (Cohen et al. 1980:5).

Although small in its beginnings and limited in its activities by the civil war (1962–70) the local development movement (*al-harika at-ta ʿawaniya*) grew in importance; in 1973, a centralized organizing body was formed in order to combine the growing volume of resources and expertise and to increase the efficiency and capacity of the various local organizations. This body was called the Confederation of Yemen Development Associations (CYDA). The legal base for the LDAs and CYDA was strengthened in 1975 and the financial sources for LDA activities were clarified and expanded. Although the LDAs were legally chartered entities under the auspices of the Ministry of

Social Affairs, Labor, and Youth, they were in fact para-statal organizations and retained a degree of semiautonomy. Their activities were regulated by a central administrative structure, and projects were planned and approved in accordance with priorities set by the government. However, these priorities were also the same as the self-reported needs of the rural people.

Efforts have continued to strengthen the LDA movement over the years and to align its activities with the central government's plans for national development. Both five-year national development plans prepared by the Central Planning Organization, 1977–81 and 1982–86, have placed considerable emphasis on the importance of the local development associations in meeting the needs of the local community, particularly in the transportation, education, and health sectors.

The local development associations were organized at four levels: local, district, governorate, and national. With the exception of the technical staff, positions in the LDA were filled through a series of elections held every three years, but only the local-level elections involved an open plebiscite to elect members of the general LDA body. The members elected to the LDA general assembly became delegates who voted for the district-level officers, the district officers later voted for officers on the governorate level, and so on.

The basic level at which the LDA was organized was the district (*nahiya*), and in some regions the subprovince (*qada'*). At this level, the LDA was composed of a general assembly and a governing Local Development Board. The size of the general assembly depended on the population of the area and the number of subdistricts (*ᶜuzlas*). It is estimated that there was one representative on the general assembly per 300–800 residents, representing the local community and directly elected to the association by the community members. The Local Development Board, responsible for management and decision making of the LDA, was elected from the general assembly and was composed of six to eight members, with three officers, a president, a general secretary, and a treasurer. In short, the LDA was the basic corporate body responsible for development activities in the district, and planning and finances were handled at this level (Cohen et al. 1980).

At the governorate level, there was a general coordinating council (*majlis it-tansiq*), which was the liaison office between the district

LDAs and the various ministries, the donor agencies, and CYDA. The *majlis it-tansiq* was made up of the presidents of the district LDAs and included the following officers: president (an honorary position assigned to the governor of the province), vice-president or general secretary, deputy secretary, and finance director. LDA projects had to be approved at the governorate level, at the planning department in CYDA, and by the relevant ministries. The coordinating council assisted in planning, financing, auditing, providing technical support, mediating disputes, and offering other institutional support to the district LDAs.

At the national level, the organization of CYDA was fairly complex. It was composed of a general assembly and an administrative board with various committees such as planning, finance, foreign relations, and cooperatives. CYDA was also organized into five departments: foreign affairs, planning and training, culture and information, administration and finance, and local development association affairs.[6] In general, CYDA's purpose was to coordinate LDA activities, offer technical and financial support, interface with the various Yemen ministries and foreign donors, oversee the success and progress of the movement, and provide standards for handling projects at the local level (e.g., supervise elections, audit financial records, and give implementation guidelines), along with ensuring that LDA projects were in accord with the national development plans as formulated by the Central Planning Organization (CPO) of the Yemen government.

Although the LDA had the authority to carry out any development project deemed appropriate by the local development board, the *majlis it-tansiq*, and CYDA, in actuality projects have been limited to infrastructure building and providing social services. In order of importance and spending, LDA projects typically included: (1) rural roads, (2) schools, (3) village water supply systems, (4) health activities (clinics, support for health staff, equipment), and (5) other miscellaneous activities such as purchase of tractors and heavy equipment, community electrification systems, operating costs, and representation expenses. Few integrated rural development projects have been undertaken by the LDA (Cohen et al. 1980:19), and cooperation between neighboring LDAs was occasionally lacking due to local and tribal disputes; but, in general, the LDAs have been quite successful in accomplishing what the central government had been incapable of doing. For example, the LDAs completed 14,679 kilometers

Table 8. Formulas for Government/Local Development Cost Sharing

Project Type		Percent Contribution		
		Local	LDA	Government
Education		33.3	33.3	33.3
Water		25.0	25.0	50.0
Health		25.0	25.0	50.0
Roads	1–20 km	(100.0	)	
(length)	20–30 km	(75.0	)	25.0
	30 + km	(25.0	)	75.0

Source: Cohen et al. 1980:17.
Note: There appear to be local variations.

of feeder roads, 4,800 classrooms, 1,334 small water projects, and 111 health projects during the period 1976–81.

Financing of LDA projects was a fairly complex matter. It usually was a mixture of local contributions, LDA tax revenues, and central government matching funds. Cohen et al. 1980 cite the formulas given in table 8 for the breakdown of LDA project costs (these are similar to formulas given to me by Anis LDA officials). The local contribution was often calculated as the worth of locally supplied labor and materials, although sometimes cash contributions were solicited.

The major source of revenue for the LDA was from the *zakat* on agricultural produce. Generally speaking, the LDA was entitled to 75 percent of the *zakat* for its operating costs and project financing. A few years ago, the LDA received the tax revenues directly through the director of finance for the region; but recently matters have been complicated, and now the *zakat* first goes to the Ministry of Finance and then is reapportioned to the LDAs on a project-by-project basis.[7]

On many projects, particularly schools and health clinics, payment of the central government matching funds was dependent on completion of the plan up to a predetermined point. For example, in the case of school construction, the building had to be completed up to the roof before it was possible to receive the Ministry of Education's matching funds, which typically covered costs for roofing material, doors, windows, furnishings, and items not locally available. Delays between completion of the local contribution and receipt of the matching funds were often quite long; thus projects sometimes stalled or were completed entirely with local resources. Other sources of revenue for the LDA included special-use taxes on LDA projects, rental of LDA-owned equipment, taxes assessed on transport of commodities, and profits on LDA activities.

Occasionally, projects were implemented through the LDA organization but entirely funded through local contribution. For example, the treasurer of the local development association in Kusma organized a scheme to improve the quality of water in the local spring-cistern system by placing polyvinyl chloride (PVC) pipe in the ancient plaster watercourse. To finance the project, each household was assessed 100 rials. The project was a failure due to inexperience in working with the PVC pipe and was sarcastically known as the *mashruᶜ al-miya* (water project, a pun on the number *miʾa*, 100, and the colloquial word *miyaʾ* for water).

Informal Community Projects

On occasion, the needs of the community cannot be met by either the central government or the LDA, in which case the local community may completely finance and implement a project on its own, in the tradition of ᶜ*ayana* (the Arabic word for cooperation), which encompasses many customary forms. The agricultural cooperation at harvest times (*jaʾish*) that is common throughout highland Yemen is a custom typifying this ethos. Other examples include pathway construction, cleaning of cisterns, and repairing public works projects. Some specific cases may illustrate this type of local development. In the community of Magharam near Kusma the need for a school was great, but the LDA was unable to assist. An elder of the community, in association with the important families (*al-ᶜayan*), organized a work force, collected money from the residents, and constructed a six-room school. In another example, the only access to the community of Shaᶜaf, Kusma, was a narrow footpath that was at times quite dangerous for the donkeys to negotiate. The community cooperated by having each family finance the segment of a widened pathway that crossed its property line while the shaykh of the region obtained contributions from the village residents who would benefit from it.[8]

Projects such as these were common throughout the western central highlands regions and are indicative of a long tradition of local cooperation in public development projects.

4

Contrasts in Development:
Jibal Rayma and Anis

There are marked differences in the rates at which local development is occurring in rural Yemen. A vivid contrast can be detected by comparing the achievements of the Anis and Jibal Rayma LDAs over their first decade of operation. This chapter examines local development in these two adjoining *qada*'s in the western central highlands, analyzing how the social, cultural, economic, and ecological conditions affect the processes of local development in rural Yemen.

Significant development in *qada* Anis began in the late 1960s and early 1970s after the uncertainties caused by the civil war subsided. The formation of the Anis LDA in 1972 allowed for the channeling of public funds into development projects. Today, Anis is one of the most developed regions in the western central highlands. *Qada* Jibal Rayma, in contrast, may be considered a local development backwater. Despite being relatively untouched by the civil war and in reasonable proximity to the port city of al-Hudayda, Jibal Rayma did not really begin rural development until 1973; even then, progress was very slow and concentrated in only a few areas. To illustrate these differences, we may review the accomplishments of the first decade of development activity for each *qada*.

DEVELOPMENT ACCOMPLISHMENTS

Roads

Despite the steep terrain, particularly in its western regions, almost every significant settlement in Anis is accessible by four-wheel-drive vehicles. The only exceptions are the smaller communities that are nestled on the shoulders of the Himyar escarpment. It is remarkable that no community in Anis is more than a few hours' hike from the nearest access road. Since the early 1970s, nearly a thousand kilometers of LDA-financed secondary roads have been carved through the *qaḍaʾ*.[1] In the first ten years of LDA operations, road construction has progressed to the point where efforts have begun to focus on widening and improving the secondary roads and on constructing links in the basic road network.

Anis is also benefiting from two major Ministry of Public Works road projects, the Maʿbar-Bajil highway, a first-class tarmac two-lane highway that will bisect Anis from west to east, and the Maʿbar/Anis rural road improvement training program. The improvement of the LDA's first road will shorten travel time throughout Anis to under two hours, linking the major district centers of Suq al-Jumaʿ, Dawran, and Maʿbar. Road construction, the number one priority of the Anis LDA, has advanced well beyond the initial stages of providing rudimentary access to the stage of improvement and maintenance.[2]

By contrast, amid quite a bit of fanfare, the first road to reach a district center in Jibal Rayma, al-Jabin, was completed in 1982. Over eight years in the making, the thirty-odd kilometer road was plagued by work stoppages and technical, funding, and property rights disputes. It was only completed as a result of increased inputs from the central government during a period when quick government access to the Jibal Rayma summit was of major strategic importance. Jibal Rayma has been able to construct just over a hundred kilometers of access roads and, with the exception of the Rabat-Jabin segment, they are of very poor quality, passable by only one vehicle at a time and subject to seasonal flooding and washouts. Only the Rabat-Jabin road, which was constructed by a professional firm, has a program of periodic maintenance that keeps it passable year-round.

Education

Anis has also made considerable progress in meeting the needs for primary education. In most of rural Yemen, primary education is a very high priority, but the construction of permanent school facilities is a slow process. To meet the immediate needs, temporary facilities such as tents, corrugated tin buildings, and unused space in larger homes have often been utilized. The overall national plan is to have a primary school (grades one through six) in each *ʿuzla* (subdistrict).

In Anis, there have been a number of accomplishments. Over fifteen new schools have been constructed with LDA participation; according to the *mudir al-mudarris* (director of schools) in Dawran, there are forty-one schooling facilities that provide over 90 percent of the *ᶜuzla*s with some kind of access to formal education.[3] Of the two dozen or so permanent schools in Anis, most are constructed using modernized variations of traditional architecture and have concrete floors, dressed stone walls, and some indoor plumbing facilities. Currently, a standardized design has been adopted for rural schools: two rows of classrooms facing a center courtyard. Classrooms are spacious and have basic but adequate furnishings. Intermediate schools are also present in the Anis district centers.

The relatively high quality of the construction of the schools in Anis is significant, because as it is indicative of the importance of education to the local communities. They are not ad hoc solutions to the education crisis, but are an indication of the planned development of rural education.

Prior to 1975, the only educational facilities in Jibal Rayma were the small Quranic schools (*maᶜhad dini*) where young students were taught to recite the Quran by rote. These schools often did not produce functional literacy. As one self-taught intellectual commented, "I studied in the *maᶜhad* and when I was through I could recite Quran but I couldn't write my name. When I was a little older, I found a copy of an Agatha Christie novel and sat and worked with it. I had learned the alphabet and this is how I taught myself to read Arabic." In 1975, the Jibal Rayma LDA financed its first education projects, building one primary school in each of the five district centers.

Since then, a few schoolhouses have been constructed in the *ᶜuzla*s, most of them through 100 percent local financing; however, only a small fraction of the *ᶜuzla*s have permanent facilities. In all, only about a dozen schools with sound roofs, blackboards, and classrooms adequate for the needs of the community have been completed. Most of the rural schools in Jibal Rayma are in fact unused buildings, often in poor repair, that have been designated as schools. Nevertheless, progress is slowly being made, largely through the efforts of a few extraordinary leaders. For example, prior to 1978 there were only 3 teachers in Kusma *nahiya* for a population of nearly 75,000. To rectify this situation, the director of schools set about obtaining as many teachers from the Ministry of Education as possible, assigning them to remote rural areas. In one year, he obtained 62 additional teachers who were placed in temporary facilities. School construction is currently on the increase in Jibal Rayma, but most are still very small and not close to the standard of those being built in Anis. As of 1982, only three of the "modern" schools (built according to Ministry of Education specifications) had been completed in Jibal Rayma. The only intermediate-level school was in the *qada'* center of al-Jabin, although there are plans for additional intermediate teachers in other districts.

Health

There are few regions in all of Yemen that have adequate rural health care coverage, and conditions are not likely to improve dramatically for some time due to the magnitude of the problem (YARG 1976*b*:21). Nevertheless, Anis has made remarkable achievements in recent years. The national plan for Yemen is designed around a hierarchical referral system; in the rural areas, there is to be at least one full health center (staffed with physicians, nurses, pharmacists, and X-ray and lab technicians in facilities equipped for minor surgical operations, outpatient clinics, and limited inpatient care) per *qada'* or serving each population of 40,000 to 50,000. In most cases, this means one health center per *nahiya*. For each population of 10,000, there should be a health dispensary (trained nurses and medical assistants); at the *cuzla* level, for each population of 2,500, there should be a primary health care unit to record vital statistics and to provide immediate first aid, simple treatment of common diseases, maternal and child care, and school and environmental health service.

In Anis, some of these goals have been exceeded, while other parts of the plan are just beginning to be implemented. Two of the three district administrative seats have health centers, and there are two additional centers in the larger market towns of Hammam ʿAli and Madinat ish-Shirq. The district center al-Jumaʿ, which is close to Madinat ish-Shirq, has a subcenter that is scheduled to be upgraded to a full health center.[4] Health posts are operational in five other market towns staffed by "unclassified" medical personnel, mostly practical nurses.

The local development association has been involved in the construction of three of the four major health centers in Anis. The large health center in Madinat ish-Shirq that was opened in 1978 was entirely LDA-financed. The other LDA health centers have been financed according to a cost-sharing scheme, with the Ministry of Health contributing roughly one-third of the cost. The subcenter in al-Juma^c is in part a private enterprise run by the local medical officer that is subsidized by the LDA, which contributes toward the rent of the building. All of the new health centers in Anis are buildings built expressly for that purpose, and all have electricity, indoor plumbing, and ample space for both outpatient and inpatient care, as well as laboratory facilities, space for X-ray equipment, and a pharmacy. The responsibility to ensure that the health centers are staffed and equipped belongs to the governorate health office (i.e., Ministry of Health), not the LDA. Unfortunately, appropriate staffing and equipping have not been completed. Nevertheless, all of the health centers at least have Yemeni and/or regional expatriate (Egyptian or Sudanese) doctors assigned to them. Although the Ministry of Health contribution for equipment and supplies has been limited, the public health component of a Netherlands government-sponsored project is helping to correct the situation. Over the first decade of LDA operations, the contribution and input of the local development association and the contributions of the local community have been consistent, and the construction of the buildings has also been of higher than average quality. In all, Anis, through local initiative and with some foreign donor support and government assistance, has taken significant steps in creating the basic physical infrastructure, particularly buildings, for providing health services in the region.

In *qadā'* Jibal Rayma, the physical infrastructure in the health sector is quite limited.[5] Only two facilities may be classified as health centers by stretching the definition. The main health center of Jibal Rayma, in al-Jabin, is actually part of an old Turkish garrison that has been cleaned up and functions as a center. The Kuwait government financed the construction of a more modern building; but, due to its inconvenient location, it has remained abandoned and is showing signs of neglect. Only one health center, located in the district administrative seat of Kusma, was constructed by the local development association. This center was instigated by the British Organization for Community Development, which provided a small grant from OXFAM to finance part of its construction. The building consists of a waiting area, an examination room/office, a dressing room, and one bathroom. There is no electricity, and running water comes from a storage tank on the roof that can be filled only during the rainy season. Furnishings are limited to a few old spring beds, one wooden couch, a desk, and some folding chairs. The building lacks medical equipment, and the doctor and two nurses assigned to the facility must use their own.

The health center in the al-Jabin garrison, a large, well-staffed, and well-furnished facility, has been the focus of a small British health team working to upgrade the services in the area and to train local birth attendants and primary health care workers. The other "health centers" in Jibal Rayma such as in Hadiya and in Bilad it-Ta ͨam make use of existing space in the district administrative seats. Across the board, health care in Jibal Rayma is limited to clinical diagnosis and minimum care.

The contrasts between health care facilities in Jibal Rayma and Anis are dramatic. In Jibal Rayma, there are no modern buildings and there has been little LDA participation or investment in health care facilities. Supplies are a problem in both areas, but in Jibal Rayma the situation is even more serious. The need for pharmaceuticals has been met by privately owned drugstores. In Jibal Rayma, most of the health care needs in the outlying areas are met by poorly trained nurses (*sahin*) operating out of their living room (*mufraj*) and, all too often, providing injections of inappropriate, useless, or even dangerous drugs. Additionally, many people still rely on itinerant healers (*muqadhdhi'in*) who practice a variety of traditional medicines, including magico-religious techniques and traditional practices such as bloodletting, cupping, and cautery.

Of course, one should not look at development in the health sector purely in terms of physical infrastructure, and development in the health manpower sector should also take into account the quality of care. Jibal Rayma has made strides in training local health workers by partially financing the operations of the British health team. Between 1978 and 1982, sixteen male village health workers had some form of training or upgrading, twelve of them receiving formal recognition by the Ministry of Health as primary health care workers. Additionally, eleven women mostly located around al-Jabin received some midwife training, and seven were accepted by the Ministry of Health as local birth attendants. Three vaccinators were also trained, and some of those mentioned above improved their skills. The results, although small, were significant and reflect some commitment to health, although the capital investment in the health sector was very low. In contrast, after its first decade of development, Anis has not benefited from an organized health care development program. Instead, it concentrated on physical infrastructure building. Local health care training, which in the 1970s was tied to the foreign assistance programs, did not become available in Anis until 1983.[6]

Agriculture

While in Jibal Rayma there are no organized agricultural projects, in Anis the Netherlands government is sponsoring a seed project aimed at improving potato production—a cash crop that is increasing in importance. As of 1982, research and training in the agricultural sector had been limited to farmers on the Maᶜbar plains on contract with three development programs to field-test the farming procedures. A British project is investigating improvements in grain production, animal husbandry, and afforestation research. The third program in Anis, also sponsored by the Netherlands, is a livestock research program aimed at improving grazing efficiency in relation to the carrying capacity of the semiarid plateau lands. Although each of these programs has an extension component, results from the basic research have yet to be translated into action, and conditions in the region have not significantly changed. The Ministry of Agriculture also has a few extension offices in the Dhamar region that provide farmers with supplies and information on fertilizer and insecticide use, but these also are fledgling activities and are not yet widely used by local farmers.

Water and Other Public Works Projects

Small water projects and rural electrification schemes are the other major public works projects undertaken through local initiative. In Anis, the LDA has undertaken over eighty projects (see table 9 for a detailed list), mostly involving the repair and maintenance of water storage facilities. The LDA has built systems for the district centers of Maᶜbar, Dawran, and al-Jumaᶜ, as well as the town of Madinat ish-Shirq. These systems involved the drilling of tube wells, placement of pipes, and construction of storage tanks. For example, in Dawran, a system with a pumping station, three kilometers of four-

Table 9. List of LDA Projects by *Qada'*, 1978–80

Anis	Jibal Rayma
Roads	
Equipment purchased: 3 cars, 1 welder, maintenance.	
Feeder roads: new or continuing construction, 27 projects; regrading, 14 projects; major repairs, 3 projects.	Feeder roads: new or continuing construction, 4 projects (2 of which were suspended).
Contribution to non-LDA roads, 4 projects.	
Education	
School construction: completion of existing plans, 8 projects; completed new schools, 5 projects; new contracts tendered, 4 projects; expansion of existing schools, 2 projects; restorations, 1 project.	Contracts tendered and new construction, 3 projects.
Contribution to non-LDA schools: new construction, 4 projects; repair, 2 projects.	
Miscellaneous: books, supplies, transportation, housing stipends.	Miscellaneous: books, supplies, transportation, housing stipends.
Health	
Improvements, upgrading, 4 projects; contracts tendered for new facilities, 2 projects.	New facilities, 1 project.
	Local training, 1 project.

Source: Anis LDA annual reports and personal observation.
Note: Period is for 1978–80 specifically. Jibal Rayma LDA did not provide reports, so data are based on personal interviews and observations.

inch pipe, and three large cement and stone cisterns was constructed by the LDA. In the more isolated rural areas, some assistance has been given to villages to construct storage tanks. In Himyar, near Dawran Anis, the LDA participated in the refurbishment of a storage dam, the construction of a large storage tank and pumping station, and the placement of approximately ten kilometers of pipe to provide drinking water for about a dozen communities surrounding the market town of Hadiqa. Additionally, a USAID project financed the drilling of a few tube wells in Qa^c Bakil, Anis, and in the construction of a rural drinking water supply system in Bani Khalid, Anis. Finally, the only real dam in the region was refurbished by the Ministry of Public Works. All of the district centers in Anis, as well as the large market towns of Hammam ^{c}Ali and Madinat ish-Shirq, have some form of municipal electricity-generating plant. Most are the result of a combination of local resources and support from central government agencies.

In Jibal Rayma, the LDA has not officially taken part in the construction of any major water systems, although a few small systems (such as in Suq ^{c}Aluja, Hadiya, and Suq Ribat) have been built by the local community. The district centers are without adequate water supplies. The major system planned for al-Jabin, piping water from a spring about three kilometers to the south of the center, was never implemented due to protracted disputes over the water rights. No municipal electricity-generating systems have been built apart from small generators to supply the government offices.

The comparison of public development in the two *qada'*s indicates significant differences in both the quantity and quality of local development projects, including those that are instigated from above as well as those based on local initiative. The remainder of this chapter analyzes why local development in the two *qada'*s was so different.

DEVELOPMENT FACTORS

Recent History

In attempting to understand the variability in rural development between Anis and Jibal Rayma, one of the first questions that might arise is whether recent historical experiences were very different in the two *qada'*s, particularly in the period immediately before the growth of the local development movement. Prior to the revolution and civil war, both Anis and Jibal Rayma were, in comparison to the other regions of Yemen, further removed from the modernizing influences of the outside world. To a large extent, the average tribesman was often unaware of or misinformed about the general conditions within Yemen, much less the rest of the world. The ʿAden trade, which has been of importance in the more cosmopolitan southern parts of the country, certainly must have had some impact on the region, especially Anis, but this was mostly concentrated in the areas adjacent to the commercial routes that crossed the Jahran plains and the track up Wadi Siham toward the main town of Dhamar.[7]

Prior to the revolution and civil war, exposure to mass media in these rural areas was limited. The transistor radio was introduced in Yemen in 1955 (Zabara 1982:28), and the distribution of the printed media was limited largely to the urban areas. Due to the high rates of illiteracy (over 90 percent), news was funneled either through the elites, most often the *sada*, or through the occasional returning traveler. The official news of the time was primarily limited to proclamations from the imam. The accounts of returning emigrants were a major source of news on outside affairs; emigration rates in the pre-revolutionary period were similar for both Anis and Jibal Rayma (YARG 1983*a*). An example of how out of touch Anis and Jibal Rayma were with the current events of the late 1950s and early 1960s can be seen in a story related to me by a shaykh in Anis.

Not long after the 1962 revolution, President Sallal (the first president of Yemen) made a trip through Anis to explain the new system of government and what it would mean for the people. In preparation for the presidential visit, the school teacher in al-Jumaʿ was ordered to instruct the small cohort of secondary school students on the revolution and new government and to send them throughout the villages to spread the news about the upcoming visit. There were only six students at that time. When the president gave his speech and he listed the atrocities committed by the imam — how he held the sons of important shaykhs of the north hostage so the powerful shaykhs would remain under his control; how he used the state treasury as his personal account; how he executed some of his own sons he thought could become potential rivals for the imamate and executed his other political rivals — the people of al-Jumaʿ were genuinely incredulous. After hearing the president's speech, people approached the students asking if the imam had really done those terrible things. The people seemed to have had little idea of the extent of the imam's repressive actions. They were only aware of his major movements, such as the time he left the country to seek medical treatment in Rome in 1959 and the attempted coup d'etat in 1955 by the imam's brother ᶜAbdullah.

In Jibal Rayma, informants related a similar situation. Most of the news of the outside world and current affairs in Yemen was channeled through the local learned elite, the *sayyids*, or the occasional returning emigrant worker. Whenever any news of importance was to be announced, the senior *sayyid* gathered the people outside his door and read and explained the report. There were always proclamations from the imam; but because there were so few radios and cosmopolitan contacts, the world view of the people of Jibal Rayma was quite parochial. As a notable example, the *sayyid* who announced the official news of the imam's government, to this date, has never left the mountain top, not even to travel to the nearest lowland regional market. What news did reach the area came by word of mouth from those who traveled to Sanaᶜa or al-Hudayda and from the migrant workers who returned from Saudi Arabia and the Gulf.

Of course, the most important recent historical event in all Yemen was the revolution and protracted civil war between 1962 and 1970. However, the disruptions caused by the uncertainties of the civil war were not felt equally in Anis and Jibal Rayma. Located in the westernmost regions of the mountains, Jibal Rayma was not directly involved in any major military campaigns. The lowland Tihama communities with which the people of Jibal Rayma carried out economic transactions, including Bayt al-Faqih, Zabid, Mansuriya, Bajil, and the port of al-Hudayda, were controlled by the republican forces; there were no serious security threats to the region posed by the royalist forces. In Jibal Rayma, no communities were demolished, no crops were decimated, and no serious damage was incurred that would require extraordinary expenses for reconstruction at the conclusion of the civil war. Although the Jibal Rayma region supported the republican cause, its contribution was limited mostly to providing manpower for the military campaigns that were carried out in the northern mountains and in the highland plains.

Anis, which extends into the plateaus in the vicinity of Maᶜbar, was more directly involved in the civil war. The towns of Dhamar and Maᶜbar were military garrisons; in 1966, a battle between the republican army and royalist forces was fought near Dawran Anis. In 1967, a battle for control of the mountain pass overlooking the main north to south highway at *Naqil* Islaᶜ, between Maᶜbar and Bilad ir-Rus, was fought. During that period, informants reported that security in the area was tenuous, and occasionally commerce between Anis and the provincial capital of Dhamar was interrupted. Nevertheless, Anis as a whole also emerged from the civil war relatively unscathed — that is, without the kind of destruction that was encountered in the northern tribal regions of Yemen. After the war, little reconstruction was needed for the area that entailed expenses that would reduce the area's ability to fund local development projects.

From the perspective of exposure to modernizing influences that resulted from participating in the military and in the revolutionary government, people from both Jibal Rayma and Anis had opportunities; but there appears to have been more direct involvement by the people from Anis in the postrevolutionary military.[8] Overall, the experiences of Anis and Jibal Rayma were quite similar in regard to the major events in recent Yemeni history. Conditions did not significantly change until after the revolution and the conclusion of hostilities in the late 1960s. To evaluate the consequences of the civil war period on development is difficult. In areas that were hard-hit, the negative effects are more calculable; but in areas such as Anis and Jibal Rayma, where direct involvement in the form of actual battle was only sporadic, the consequences are less clear. On one hand, it is evident that the cooperative movement was hamstrung; formalized self-help organizations did not really become effective until after the war. On the other hand, some activity, such as the construction of a few kilometers of access roads to facilitate troop movements, may have been quite beneficial, providing a basis for local development. In this sense, Anis was in an advantageous position to benefit from the few kilometers of the main road bulldozed during the civil war period; Jibal Rayma had no roads until 1976, when construction on the Ribat-Jabin road began. However, neither area engaged in any significant rural development until after the revolution. Therefore, from the perspective of recent historical events, Anis and Jibal Rayma had approximately the same start on the path of rural development and were affected or not affected, as the case may be, by the same regional influences.

Center-Periphery Relations

In considering the possible factors affecting local development, particularly in regard to external influences, the relation of the rural community to the urban center is important. Proximity and the accompanying social, political, and economic ties to the urban center often provide a direct stimulus to development activities. The two *qada*'s in this analysis vary in the nature of their relations to the urban centers. Anis, located in the eastern portion of the western central highlands region, has maintained close ties to the regional capital of Dhamar as well as to the capital city of Sanaᶜa. Jibal Rayma is in close proximity to the port city of al-Hudayda and the regional towns of Bayt al-Faqih and Mansuriya in the Tihama. In terms of travel time, both *qada*'s are about an hour's drive from the main cities (as measured from the closest point). From an economic perspective, each area was within the sphere of a major urban area. Jibal Rayma historically had ties to al-Hudayda, where it exchanged its coffee and qat production, and Anis was closely tied to the markets of Dhamar and Sanaᶜa. The major difference was in the relationships between the *qada*'s and the seats of power. Anis was very near the governorate capital of Dhamar and less than a hundred kilometers from Sanaᶜa. Jibal Rayma had just the opposite situation. It was many days' journey to the governorate offices in Sanaᶜa. Furthermore, since virtually all of the ministerial and national political offices as well as the head offices of the Confederation of Yemen Development Associations are in Sanaᶜa, it was particularly difficult for Jibal Rayma to maintain close contacts. Although economically and militarily very important, the port city of al-Hudayda did not have many administrative branch offices of the major ministries until the middle 1970s. By being more closely linked with the capital city, Anis was much more involved in national politics and able to draw from the modern services available, facts that undoubtedly worked to its advantage in developing the LDA.

Geographical Conditions

Another important area to explore in rural development is the barrier imposed by topographical and geographical conditions. A rule commonly noted in rural Yemen is that development progresses in relationship to improvements in transportation (Young, et al. 1981). Lengths of pipe for water supply systems, cement mixers and quality building timber for schools and clinics, drilling rigs for artesian wells, and tractors and four-wheel-drive vehicles for farming and marketing are all dependent on access roads. Once a primary road is cut, other development activities then follow at an accelerated pace. As may be expected, difficulty in road construction is closely associated with the nature of the terrain; this raises the question of the constraints on local development that may be attributed to ecological and topographical conditions.

Western visitors to Anis often note its similarity to the American southwest tablelands. However, the area most accessible to the occasional traveler is the eastern part of the *qada'* near the highland central plateau, a region crossed by the main north to south highway connecting Sana^ca to Ta^ciz. In fact, only about one-fifth of Anis is in the high plains zone. In the two main plains, Qa^c Jahran and Qa^c Bakil, most of the roads were created either through repeated use by four-wheel-drive vehicles and medium-sized trucks or through light grading with a bulldozer. The other four-fifths of Anis, extending from the plains to the west, is rugged mountainous terrain. These mountainous areas, which include Hayad Manar, Jabal ish-Shirq, and western Dawran, have been the focus of most of the rural road construction by the local development association. Road construction in the plains was technically simple, so the LDA placed its initial emphasis on opening up the mountainous regions where the largest part (80 percent) of the population of the *qada'* lives.

To illustrate the difficulty of mountain road building in Anis, we may look at the problems encountered in constructing the main road (about ninety kilometers in length) that connects the main market town of Madinat ish-Shirq in Wadi Rima^c to Suq al-Juma^c on the summit of Jabal ish-Shirq to Dawran Anis and Ma^cbar in the plains (see map 3). Five main mountain passes had to be crossed, requiring extensive blasting and earth moving. The segment of road between Madinat ish-Shirq and Suq al-Juma^c involved an elevation gain of about 1,100 meters in about ten kilometers; immediately northeast of al-Juma^c, the pass at *Naqil* Sitran was a sheer slope of about 800 meters that required construction of a sinewy, switchback road. In all, about two-thirds, or sixty kilometers, of the Anis road was cut through the rugged mountains of the western central highlands. The construction task was not, by any means, a simple one. This initial road project was the main objective of the LDA for its first three years of operations.

Jibal Rayma is almost entirely mountainous (see map 4). The western slopes, which rise sharply from the Tihama plains to over

2,500 meters, are among the highest and steepest in all of Yemen, while the eastern and southern slopes are more gradual and are crossed by medium-sized wadis. The main road construction effort has been on the "official" road between Suq Ribat, at the base of the western flank (600 meters) and the *qada'* capital of al-Jabin (2,300 meters). This road was started in the mid-1970s and was not completed until July of 1982. Although it is about twenty-five kilometers in length with an elevation gain of 1,500 meters, it took an exceptionally long time to construct.

Physical constraints were a major problem in Jibal Rayma; in comparison to the Anis road, the Jibal Rayma road was definitely more difficult to construct on a kilometer-per-kilometer basis. The slope of Jibal Rayma is steeper that Anis, and the elevation gain higher. However, the distance was much shorter. The main problem with the Jibal Rayma road was due not to the technical difficulties encountered along the way, but to a prolonged work stoppage caused by problems in funding and by strong protests from farmers arising from the damages done to the terraced slopes. At issue was the question of eminent domain and just compensation; as we shall see, the route required the destruction of some coffee terraces. The problems of obtaining the right-of-way may also have been exaggerated because the destruction of coffee terraces was in some ways symbolic of the destruction of the old power structure (a point explored in chapter 5). Between 1978 and 1980, the road progressed only about five kilometers (see map 5). Once work began in earnest between 1980 and 1982, and there were no more local interruptions, the remaining two-thirds of the road was quickly completed.

The completion of the road coincided with the rising political tensions in the region. The leftist National Democratic Front was active in the eastern and southern regions of the district, and it became important to be able to bring additional military troops into the region, so government pressure was brought to bear to speed up the completion of the project. The road to the district center and the military garrison now had strategic importance, so an award was reportedly offered by the president of the republic to the first car to reach the summit (which was in fact dragged to the top by a bulldozer) as an additional incentive to complete the project. It was only when the road became an important factor in the security of the region that progress rapidly increased. It is evident that the road that took over six years to complete could have been done in a much shorter period had it not been subject to repeated work stoppages.

From a technical perspective, both the initial Anis road and the Jibal Rayma road from Suq Ribat to al-Jabin presented serious difficulties. But four-fifths of Anis is similar to Jibal Rayma, and the mountainous regions in Anis were the site of the main road construction activities. As the example of road construction indicates, geographical differences between the two regions had an effect on the pace at which development projects were completed. However, the similarities in the two regions far outweigh the differences; both areas faced enormous barriers in constructing the rural roads that were the first and basic step in development of the regions. Especially telling is the fact that the Jibal Rayma road progressed rapidly once there was a mandate to put aside disputes and concentrate on construction. This clearly indicates that factors other than environmental constraints were also influencing the processes of development.

Economic Factors

Economic conditions carry the potential directly to affect rural development programs that require a large local contribution. It was noted above that work on the main road in Jibal Rayma was often stopped due to local political disputes and problems involving the release of funds allocated to the project. The projects of Anis, however, did not seem to run into such difficulties. The main road, the health clinics, and the schools were completed almost on schedule, without unnecessary delays.[9]

The economy of the highland rural areas in the 1970s was dramatically affected by the large input of cash from emigration and expatriate remittances. Steffen and Geiser note that "as the remittances of the Yemeni labor force abroad often represent the main source of cash income, the relative wealth of many areas of Yemen is in direct proportion to the emigration rates" (1977:22). Local initiative development is dependent on locally generated tax revenues and community contributions; thus, it is important to inquire into the differences in local economic situations, particularly as they relate to emigration patterns and agricultural production.

The economic boom in Yemen was fueled largely through expatriate cash remittances. Therefore, some inferences on the economic situation in each *qada'* can be drawn from examination of the rates of emigration. Table 10 presents the rates for the two regions as calculated for each *qada'* from both the 1975 and 1981 censuses. Both areas show relatively low emigration rates in the mid-1970s and then a dramatic jump by 1981, and the differences between the two areas are not significant. Both regions benefited greatly from the increased cash infused into the local economy by migrants during the late 1970s. Assuming that the rates of remittances do not vary significantly between regions (and there is no reason to believe otherwise), the availability of cash resulting from remittances that could be funneled into the funding of development programs was similar in the two regions.

Local cash contributions, like those made available from expatriate remittances, account for one-third of the financial input on local development projects, and revenues derived from the agricultural *zakat* (tax) allocated to the LDAs make up another one-third. In order to get an indication of the tax base from which these *qada*'s could finance their programs, it is therefore important to compare the agricultural production of the two regions. Although actual figures for tax collection are not available, reasonably reliable inferences can be drawn by extrapolating from the area of land under cultivation.

The three main crops that are important sources of *zakat* revenue are cereals, coffee, and qat. The most important of these is quite possibly qat, due to its high market value and its wide cultivation. Qat figures have not been included in the national accounts since the early 1970s, although it is undoubtedly the most valuable crop in the agricultural sector. Table 11 presents the approximate area under cultivation for each of the main crops. Clearly, the most significant difference here between Anis and Jibal Rayma is in the area under cereal cultivation. Anis has more than three times the area under production. However, most of this area is in the highland plains, subject to high winds and lower rainfall levels that give substantially reduced yields when compared with the western-facing mountain slopes.

For qat and coffee, which are the most important cash crops, the areas under cultivation are roughly similar. Jibal Rayma, located to the west of Anis, receives slightly more rainfall. An important difference is that during the drier winter months Jibal Rayma also has

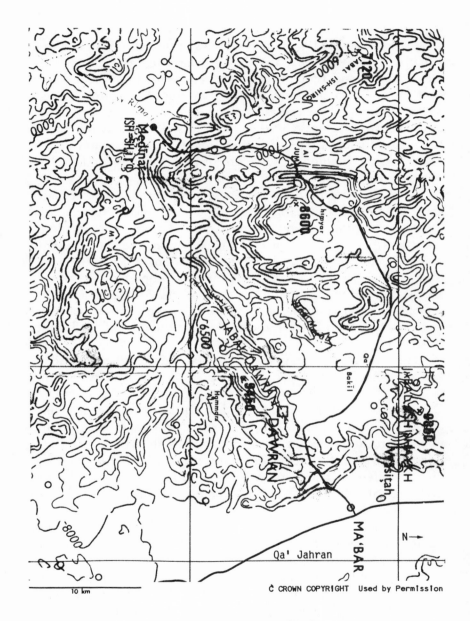

Map 3. Contour map of Anis

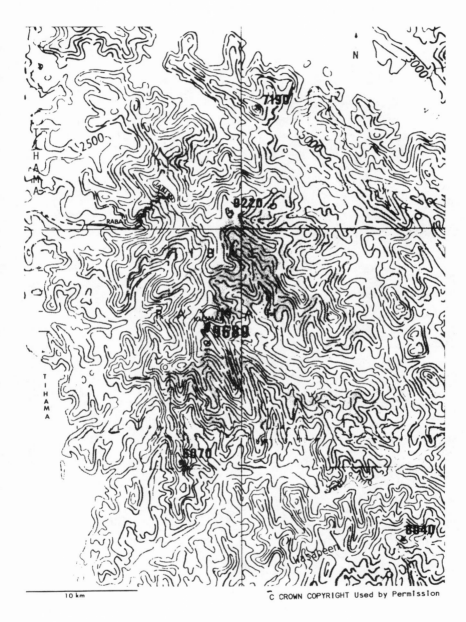

Map 4. Contour map of Jibal Rayma

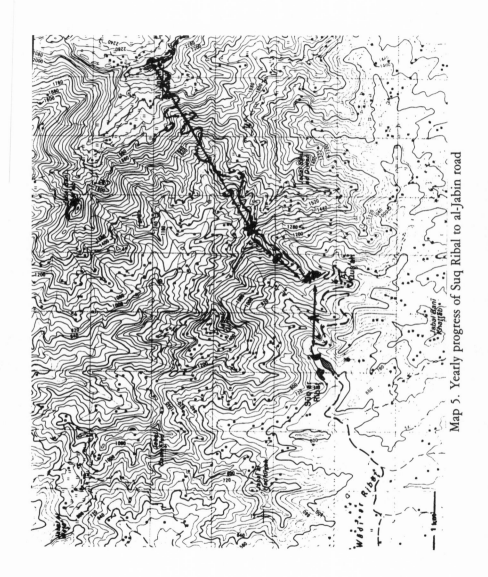

Map 5. Yearly progress of Suq Ribal to al-Jabin road

Table 10. Emigration Rates of Anis and Jibal Rayma

1975 Swiss Technical Cooperation Census			
Anis		*Jibal Rayma*	
Number of Emigrants	Rate	Number of Emigrants	Rate
4,064	3.72	6,368	3.99
Population: 109,231		159,720	
1981 CYDA Census			
Anis		*Jibal Rayma*	
Number of Emigrants	Rate	Number of Emigrants	Rate
35,762	20.3	47,934	18.9
Population: 176,175		253,554	

Source: Swiss Technical Cooperation 1977; CYDA census.
Note: The emigration rate = emigrants × 100/(inhabitants + emigrants).

Table 11. Approximate Area under Cultivation (in Hectares)

	Anis			*Jibal Rayma*	
Qat	Coffee	Cereals	Qat	Coffee	Cereals
2,680	3,820	72,105	2,106	3,019	22,023

Source: Revri 1983.

afternoon cloud cover and fog that helps to reduce drought damage and support higher yields of coffee and qat than in Anis, thereby offsetting the small differences in area under cultivation.

Table 12 presents a rough estimate of the tax potential for each *qada'* that may serve as the base for calculating the potential for locally generated development association project funding. The estimate was made by taking the area under production and calculating a potential tax figure based on the average gross margin for each of the main crops.[10] In his recent study on qat and agricultural production, Revri has determined that, on a national average, the gross-margin per hectare of qat is 213,900 rials; for coffee, 13,180 rials; and for sorghum, the main cereal crop, 6,290 rials (1983:84). To get a reasonable estimate, the *zakat* rate of 10 percent, which is the rate for rain-fed lands, is used to assess the tax potential for the cereal crops, while the lower 5 percent rate for irrigated lands is used to

Table 12. Estimated Tax Potential for Jibal Rayma and Anis

	Anis	Jibal Rayma
Qat	1,146,504 YR	900,947 YR
Coffee	2,517,380 YR	1,989,521 YR
Cereals	45,354,045 YR	13,852,467 YR

Source: Revri 1983.
Note: Based on 1980 figures for gross margin of the main crops and *zakat* rate of 10 percent for cereals, 5 percent for coffee, and 0.02 percent for qat.

calculate the totals for coffee.[11] Table 12 presents rough estimates of the tax potential for the two *qada*'s.

Although it is uncertain precisely how much of the potential tax revenue from qat is actually realized, an immediately striking feature is the tenfold difference in gross margins between qat and the other crops and the high level of income generated for the farmer from qat cultivation in comparison to other crops. Calculations based on observations in one of the regional markets in Kusma *nahiya* support Revri's high estimates of the revenue-generating potential of qat. The *wakil* of the qat suq in Kusma estimated that, on a daily average, . . . qat worth from 20,000 to 25,000 rials was sold in this one market; and on Thursday suq day, the amount was close to 100,000 rials. On an average day, about 50 *shikla* (bundles of eight *rubta*s) of qat were sold at an average price of 30 rials per *rubta*. Averaged over a year, this totals 3,756,000 rials. Adding the Thursday market estimates of one 100,000 rials per day, the yearly total estimate for one market is 8,956,000 rials. The 10 percent sales tax on this amount of qat yields a total of nearly 900,000 rials, of which 2 percent or about 18,000 YR is allocated to the LDA account.[12]

Of course, it is highly unlikely that the actual tax realized is as high as the potentials indicated in table 12, but even if it is only half that amount, it is clear that in terms of agricultural production both Anis and Jibal Rayma have large tax bases to work with. An interesting result from the calculation of the potential tax revenues for Anis and Jibal Rayma is that the tax potential in Anis was much higher than what was actually reflected in the LDA accounts; Anis should have had a much larger LDA annual budget than Jibal Rayma. One interpretation to explain this oddity is that the people of Jibal Rayma are more conscientious in meeting their *zakat* obligations (and therefore their LDA contributions), while the people in Anis are not as interested in supporting the LDA. However, this seems to contradict the large body of evidence that the people of Anis fully supported their LDA. An alternative explanation, one that is supported by local interpretations of the political situation, that may account for the differences in the willingness to fulfill tax obligations is that the people in Anis and Jibal Rayma exhibit different attitudes and behavior toward government authorities. Although a percentage of *zakat* revenues is eventually allocated to the LDA, it is nevertheless collected by government officers—the *mudir al-mal* and his assistants, usually the community secretaries (*amins*). Tax collection is perceived as the government dipping into the individual household accounts. In Anis, as in many other tribal areas in Yemen, the authority of the central government in local affairs is comparatively weak and generally regarded as a form of interference. This is supported by the fact that other branches of the central government administrative structure, such as the mediating role of the *mudir's* office, are comparatively underutilized (see chapter 5). Tax collection is associated with government penetration in local affairs; withholding of tax contributions is seen as limiting the government interference and is therefore not directed at the LDA per se.

By contrast, in Jibal Rayma the central government has considerable influence and power in local affairs. Central government officers such as the *mudir* are very active, and the power of the central government is feared. One local leader expressed his amazement at how merely a note from the *mudir* causes fear and trepidation among the people of Jibal Rayma, whereas in the east (i.e., Anis) nobody pays the government (*hukuma*) any mind. When the *mudir al-mal* and his agents, as representatives of the government, make tax assessments and demand payment, the people of Jibal Rayma defer to their authority. Consequently, the tax potential of Jibal Rayma is more fully realized than in Anis; but this is more a function of the relations between the people and the central government authorities than a reflection of attitudes toward community participation in local development activities.

The principal point of the argument in this section is that neither area was agriculturally impoverished and without potential local resources that could be channeled into development activities. Furthermore, when comparing the actual local development association budgets between the two *qada*'s, the differences are minimal. For the year 1978–79, Anis LDA had a budget of just under 2,000,000 rials (Anis LDA Annual Report 1978–79). An informant in Kusma reported that for the year 1978–79 Kusma's LDA also had a budget of 2,000,000 rials. [13]

Both areas actually were able to collect similar sums of money for their development associations, which is further evidence that economic conditions, while important in determining the overall level of development activity, are not, in this case, the critical factor differentiating the two *qada*'s of Jibal Rayma and Anis. The economic evidence indicates that both areas were capable of funding local level development; but, as noted, Anis was better able to translate this potential into action. This suggests that other factors besides the local economic situations were influencing the process of development in the two regions, which may account for the differences observed. The problem of local development in this region appears not so much one of affording development activities, but rather of the organization and implementation of local development.

Having accounted for the similarities in the two cases and suggested that the most reasonable explanation for the differences in local development may lie within the social and political arena, the following chapters turn to a fuller examination of how these two cases contrast and what other kinds of factors were important in the local development process.

5

Social Organization and Power

Understanding the rural sociopolitical organization in Jibal Rayma and Anis requires an appreciation of Yemen's historical circumstances. As Chelhod (1970) has noted, Yemen developed its social system from a Bedouin past in which social organization was based on the tribal model.[1] The new sedentary life of the Bedouin tribes and the development of agriculture necessitated modifications in the systems, changes that reflected the importance of land ownership and fixed and recognized territorial boundaries. As a consequence, the emphasis on kinship as the defining feature of the tribe was lessened, and tribal membership became more a matter of a political allegiance coupled with residence within a specific territory. In sketching the outline of Yemen social organization, there are three different types of institutions—the tribe, the segmentary lineage system, and the state administrative system. All three to one extent or another play an important role in regulating public action and therefore are of importance in understanding rural development.

Describing these systems of sociopolitical organization is further complicated because there is often a good deal of overlap between them. The current state administrative divisions were often drawn up according to the preexisting tribal boundaries and groupings; a tribe is often isomorphic with a state administrative division, and a tribal subsection may be isomorphic with both a maximal lineage and a local administrative division. Furthermore, the presence of administrative divisions such as the *qada'*, left over from the Otto-man Turks and other administrations, complicates the picture. We may consider the traditional tribal system to be the base sketch over which layers of administrative divisions and political divisions based on territorial concerns have been added. Finally, the composite for Yemen is one with a great deal of regional variation. This discussion of social organization begins with a review of the major divisions in the tribal system.

TRIBAL ORGANIZATION

Historically, there were three principal Yemeni tribal confederations — Hashid, Bakil, and Mathij; however, only the first two still retain significance. The confederation represents a system of alliances between specific tribes. It is a loose political constellation that acts together at times when a unified tribal position is needed to create an image of strength and solidarity. The confederation may become important when conflict arises, as a political action group when economic interests are threatened, or if there are pressing reasons to try to influence national-level policies. At the level of the confederation of tribes, leadership is vested in the paramount shaykh.[2] Although of great importance in the Zaydi regions to the north and east of the capital city Sanaᶜa, the confederation is only important in certain sections of the western central highlands.

The Tribe

In the western central highlands, the tribes are referred to as *qabila* (pl. *qaba'il*) and are essentially political entities. When one speaks of a tribe, one is referring both to a specific area and to the people who live within it. "The tribe and the territory it inhabits are coterminous" (Adra 1982:18). Although there is considerable scholarly debate over the nature of the Yemeni tribes, at a minimum they are named political entities that play an important role in the regulation of public affairs. As Dresch (1984:33–34) has pointed out, most tribes have deep historical roots and are associated with specific territories. The tribesmen relate to each other in a genealogical idiom; members of the same tribe address each other as "brother" and rationalize this putative kinship through reference to a common tribal eponym. Typically, one finds tribal segments with names such as Bani Fadl, Dhu Hussayn, ᶜIyal Yazid, and the like, all reflecting a notion of common ancestry (e.g., ᶜIyal Yazid literally means dependents of Yazid). However, this tribal relatedness is merely a statement of a common political identity expressed in a genealogical idiom, not a detailing of actual kinship relationships. It is quite common to find tribal units that are composed of one or two descent groups, but the members of the larger tribal units are related only in the abstract. While one may choose a tribal affiliation by moving into another area, people are, for the most part, simply born into a tribe and retain this tribal affiliation throughout their life.

Tribal structure is segmentary—that is, tribes are composed of sections, subsections, subsubsections, and so on; the actual number of levels can vary. The levels of segmentation have no specific name, but often they are labeled "fifths," "fourths," "eighths," and the like. To illustrate this rather abstract description, we may add the spatial dimension; a subsection might include ten or twenty villages spread out over a 20- or 25-square-kilometer area, depending, of course, on the ecological conditions. A section may extend across a hundred square kilometers or so, include four or five subsections, and total five or ten thousand people. A tribe is made up of a number of sections, covering hundreds of square kilometers and numbering thirty or forty thousand members.

Named segments may be represented by one or more shaykhs, depending on the size of the segment; some segments have no shaykhs at all, and others have many. Individuals are free to take their problems to any shaykh they wish, but most often it is expedient to deal with the local shaykh, especially if he also happens to be a close kinsman.

Tribal membership is also associated with a powerful ideology, an ethos that prescribes proper canons of moral behavior and reciprocal obligations.[3] Again, there is debate on just how much responsibility there is among tribesmen to come to each other's assistance, and practical considerations often play an important role; nevertheless, the ideology of unity is a strongly felt motivating force.[4]

THE LINEAGE STRUCTURE

Along with the segmentary system of tribal political units, there is a segmentary lineage kinship system. Because both the tribal and kinship systems employ a genealogical idiom (i.e., use terms like "brother" and "son" and make reference to ancient ancestors) to characterize their relationships, care must be taken not to merge the two systems. The kinship system is a mechanism for forming social groups obligated by virtue of actual common descent traced through the male line. At the very lowest levels of association (i.e., from the nuclear family up to the minimal agnatic units), these are clearly defined entities that are often corporate in nature. However, as the genealogical distance increases and the relationships become more abstract, the confusion over just how the system is structured and what constitutes a lineage subunit increases (Chelhod 1970; Stevenson 1981; Adra 1982).[5] A large lexicon exists to refer to these lineage divisions, but often the terms overlap, have multiple meanings, or simply refer to different levels of segmentation according to local usage. "Stomach" (*batn*), "branch" (*fakhdh*), "meat" (*lahma*), "house" (*bayt*), and "sinew" (*habl*) all are rather organic terms for lineage divisions above the level of the extended household.[6] "*Lahma* is simply the clan, made up of a number of lineages called *badana* or *ᶜasaba*. The *habl* (sinew) is the genealogical *claim* which allows one to go back to the founding ancestor of the lineage and determine the place occupied by each of the descendants in relation to the group. It boils down to the line of descent. Finally, the *ᶜusrat* seems to merge with the patriarchal family" (Chelhod 1979:51; emphasis added).

Disagreement over the terminology used in discussions of lineage relations can be seen by contrasting Chelhod's description with that of Stevenson, who worked in a nearby area. Stevenson finds that the maximal agnatic group is referred to as *bayt*, while *habl* refers to an alliance group consisting of closely related minimal lines (1981:102–15). Where Chelhod finds *habl* to be a term referring to the *principle* of patrilineal descent—that is, the genealogical linking—Stevenson finds it to be a term that defines a *type* of descent group.[7] "In theory, the *habl* was collectively responsible for the major public obligation of its members. These included debts (blood money or *diya*) in the event of a murder, accidental death, or other major offenses. As well, the *habl* was supposed to support its members in disputes, to line up with them" (Stevenson 1985:72).

In fact, attempts to present a concise, clear-cut description of just which kinsmen belong to what lineage subdivisions are largely futile because the native model is itself flexible. The segmentary model is the statement of a principle for the formation of larger groups when and if the need arises; it is not a definition of concise genealogically defined political entities. As Adra argues, "It [the segmentary model] provides both the mind set and the rationale to bring diverse individuals together without necessitating coercion or the centralization of power. It is not intended, however, to define all possible relationships involving mutual rights and obligation" (1982:115). In daily affairs, the sociopolitical importance of the larger descent groups is only rarely demonstrated and then mostly in an ad hoc manner. These descent groups come together in times of ritual or crisis when collective action is needed, such as in the cases of blood feud, economic disaster, or threat from outside forces; the existence of kin-based corporate groups is generally limited to the level of the minimal agnatic groups.

More importance appears to be placed on the responsibilities and loyalties owed to the tribal groups with whom one resides than on loyalty to one's descent group. Informants in the western central highlands, when posed the hypothetical question of loyalty should a conflict arise between two tribal groups, stated that the tribesman was obliged to side with the group with whom he resided even if the opposing group was his descent group. Residency was made analogous to citizenship and was more important than kinship. When a family emigrated into another tribal area, a fairly common event in the western central highlands, a formal agreement was made with the host group pledging loyalty in order to ensure security, shared responsibilities, and the benefits of group membership. It was said that, if one did not make the agreement, the right to purchase land was denied or the family was simply left to fend for itself in times of trouble. This would create a perilous existence.

THE STATE ADMINISTRATIVE SYSTEM

Since the revolution, the development of a state administrative structure has had increased impact on local political and economic affairs. Local development activities must interface with this state administrative system and the local political entities. Therefore, it is important to outline the basic features of the local administrative divisions of the state system.

The Subprovince (*Qada'*)

The *qada'* is an administrative unit that is a holdover from the Turkish administration; currently, it is of little importance in the government system, apart from occasional use in census activities and in agricultural research. There are no state or local government offices specifically designated for the *qada'*, yet it does retain some importance. *Qada'* is a term used to refer to a grouping of districts or *nahiya*s. It also makes sense as an administrative unit that frequently correlates with either geographical or tribal boundaries. For example, in the western central highlands, *qada'* Anis is in fact the tribe of Anis. It consists of three *nahiya*s—Ma°bar/Jahran, Dawran, and Jabal ish-Shirq. In Anis, the boundaries of the *qada'* and the tribe are identical. The *qada'* was a recognized unit for cooperative action in local development. Until 1982, districts could combine their resources, using the *qada'* as the administrative unit to define their local development association. This was often done in the western central highlands. Since there are limited governmental resources to provide full services (such as courts, secondary and intermediary schools, health facilities, rural police and security forces), the *qada'* center has a higher concentration of services.

The District (*Nahiya*)

The *nahiya*, like the *qada'*, is a territorial administrative unit that represents the furthest penetration of the central government into local politics (Cohen et al. 1980:4). Like the *qada'*, the *nahiya* is an administrative unit that tends to correspond to tribal boundaries. It is the most important administrative division in the rural areas; all governmental services are organized according to *nahiya*. The affairs of the *nahiya*s are directed by a government-appointed official (*mudir an-nahiya*) who acts as general supervisor of the region, controls the police and security, and serves as mediator in local disputes that cannot be handled by the shaykhs or other locally recognized leaders.

Officials and offices in the *nahiya* center usually include a director of finance (*mudir al-mal*) who overseers tax collection and governmental expenditures in the district; a director of security with a small contingent of soldiers; a director of schools; and the district courts presided over by an appointed judge.

Local Divisions

The Subdistrict (°*uzla*s)
The °*uzla* is the smallest unit in the official state system of administrative divisions. It should be emphasized that the °*uzla*s are specifically administrative divisions that were originally structured to facilitate taxation. Therefore, the size of these units is fairly uniform

across the entire western central highlands region. In the tribal areas, the *ʿuzla*s were drawn up with tribal boundaries in mind, but they are not necessarily replicas of the tribal territories. For example, a large tribal segment may be subdivided into a number of *ʿuzla*s, but an *ʿuzla* will not crosscut two tribal segments. There may be an overlap with tribal divisions; frequently, the locality that is recognized as the *ʿuzla* is in fact also a tribal segment. The situation varies from area to area, and no hard and fast rules apply. In many localities, the tribesmen elect not to refer to such areas as *ʿuzla*s, and substitute other terms, such as *rubuʿ* or *mikhlaf*. Each *ʿuzla* elects an official secretary (*amin*) who is a deputy of the *nahiya* director of finance. His chief duty is that of tax assessor and collector and official secretary of minor administrative matters. The *amin* is an elected official and may receive about 1 percent of the tax for his services.

Village Clusters

In the mountainous regions of Yemen, dwellings are scattered throughout the countryside, sometimes heavily concentrated and sometimes isolated. Concentrated settlements may be known as villages (*qura*, singular *qarya*) or hamlets (*mahalat*, singular *mahal*), with the *qarya* usually being distinguished because of the presence of a small suq. Village clusters that are represented by a shaykh, *amin*, or *ʿaql* are known variously as *thuman*, *mugharam*, *madhbatat*, or *mamasi* depending on the region. They are usually composed of a limited number of descent groups and therefore are integrated by kinship ties. The individual villages or hamlets are generally represented by an elder *ʿaql* who is spokesman for the group. These local units are named, though quite often the name does not reflect the identity of the descent group or groups who live there. These are the lowest level of officially recognized units and frequently have their own secretary responsible for tax assessment and collection.

The Household (*Bayt, Daʾima*)

The smallest unit is the extended household, sometimes referred to as the *bayt* or *daʾima*, made up of one or more nuclear families (*ʿusar*). The household is locally defined as those who share the same kitchen—that is, who take meals together and are united as one domestic unit. They often engage in farming as a single entity and share household duties.

Having outlined the general structure of the three modes of social organization, we may now see how they are manifest in each of the two areas.

SOCIAL ORGANIZATION

Anis

Anis is a very large tribe numbering just over 100,000 people. Its territory is spread out over a vast area that includes the three administrative districts Dawran, Jabal ish-Shirq, and Ma'bar/Jahran. Like many of the northern tribes (Dresch 1984:33), Anis demonstrates a segmentary structure; however, there is not a good deal of symmetry between the segments in the system. Although Anis is not included among the scholarly lists of the generally recognized Yemeni tribes, Anis considers itself a member of the Bakil federation.[8] The tribe of Anis is made up of a number of large segments with considerable historical depth composed, in turn, of smaller subsections; the segments may vary in size and number. Often the larger segments are referred to as *mikhlafs*. Each *mikhlaf*, as well as each of the lower levels of segmentation, is associated with a shaykh. The shaykh of the *mikhlaf* is in actuality the shaykh of a lower-level segment who has gained a reputation and acquired a wide clientele. For example, the shaykh of Bani Hatim is first of all the shaykh of the tribal "fifth" named as-Sayh. The larger segments number about 10,000 people, while the smaller subsections average around 1,500 members; the smaller segments contain an average of eleven villages.

The names of the tribal segments generally reflect the genealogical idiom, but this is not observed in all cases. The names of the major tribal segments such as Bani Hatim, Himyar, and Bani Khalad indicate a genealogical basis for membership in the tribal segment, but actual kinship links to the "apical" ancestors are not maintained. For example, one of the "fifths" of Himyar, Bani Fadl, is a segment that consists of about 2,000 people; but Bani Fadl is actually composed of two large descent groups, al-'Atif and Tamish. The al-'Atif claim some ancient links to the Bakil tribes near the ab-Bawn area north of Sana'a, and the Tamish claim to have come from "somewhere near al-Jawf" in the arid northeast of the country. Rather than being the name of a known historical progenitor of the tribal

segment, Bani Fadl is the political name of the tribal segment; there
are no specific "descendants" of an ancient ancestor named Fadl, and
no stories to indicate any historical connection. In this regard, the
tribal system in Anis is much like the system described by Dresch
(1984) for the more northern tribes. The tribal segments are basically
political, rather than kinship entities. In Anis, the members of the
tribal segments tend to be closely related, as the example from Bani
Fadl indicates.

The major tribal segments in Anis cover rather large areas, but
they are not all equal in size. For example, Bani Salama covers over
350 square kilometers, while the territory of Himyar includes around
175 square kilometers. A typical subsection in Anis, Bani Fadl, incorporates about 12 square kilometers and numbers about 2,400 residents who live in sixteen villages.

To be an Anis tribesman, it is sufficient to assert a general claim
of descent from one of the ancient tribes. Theoretically, individuals
may shift tribal membership, but this appears to be an infrequent
occurrence. The main reason inhibiting frequent shifts in tribal membership is that tribal boundaries are very closely guarded. Each tribal
segment in Anis is associated with a territory over which it holds
general proprietary rights. Private property is recognized; however,
tribal territory is considered the sum total of all lands—private
(*milk*), religiously endowed (*waqf*), and public (*himi*, *fish*). If an
individual merely shifts tribal affiliation, without selling his land
and moving, it means that the generalized rights over his lands are
taken away from the tribal segment, thereby effecting a realignment
of tribal boundaries. Alliance shifting is seen as an alienation of
tribal lands, and this is very strongly resisted. The tribal boundaries
have been more or less stable over time; they have a historical life
above that of the individual property holders.

Of equal importance, the identity of the tribal segment is closely
tied to the land. If the land is alienated to different segments, then
the identity of the tribal segment is weakened and eventually may
disappear. An individual is free to sell his land and move, reestab-
lishing membership in another tribe or tribal segment by signing a
formal agreement, but he is not free to shift his alliance—not without running the risk of encountering violent resistance. Strong forces
mitigate against individuals selling land to a member of another
tribal group unless the new owner is willing to join the segment. A

Khums al-Haql
Khums as-Sayh
Khums al-Wasat   ············Bani Hatim
Khums al-Kharim
Khums al-Halal

(similar   ... Bani Khalad
subdivisions)   ... Mikhlaf al-Jabal   .... Anis
               ... Bani Salama

Khums Bani Fadl
Khums Bani Saqi
Khums al-Hibs   ············Himyar
Khums al-Wasat
Khums Huzayn

Figure 2. Anis tribal segments: Example from Dawran

few examples from Anis indicate how closely territorial boundaries are maintained.

In the community of Maghrabit al-ʿAnis, located in eastern Jabal ish-Shirq, Anis, an armed conflict erupted when Mr. M tried to switch his tribal affiliation from *mikhlaf* al-Hada' to *mikhlaf* Bani Khalad in the *nahiya* of Dawran, Anis. The household of Mr. M was located right on the border between the two districts, which also happened to be the border between the two tribal segments. The house was situated on a lofty perch overlooking the settlements of Maghrabit al-ʿAnis in the valley. Although originally belonging to Maghrabit al-ʿAnis, with consanguineal ties to this group, Mr. M decided to shift alliance; his reasons were that most of his economic transactions were with Bani Khalad and the only road access to his home was through that area. Furthermore, he was living on top of a steep hill and the plans to run a roadway from Maghrabit al-ʿAnis up the slope and through Bani Khalad had been scrapped, so he felt it expedient to make the change. Anytime he wished to come or go, he had to travel through Bani Khalad territory, and not al-Hada', so he felt it in his best interests formally to recognize an affiliation with his neighbors over whose land he "trespassed" nearly every day. In making this shift, he laid claims to the undeveloped lands below his house, extending to the valley floor and including one important spring. The residents of Maghrabit al-ʿAnis in the valley floor opposed the transfer because it would reapportion their boundary and mean the loss of hectares of grazing and firewood foraging grounds and an important source of water and leave them in a strategically vulnerable position. The attempt to transfer his alliance and property to Bani Khalad was seen as an affront to the collective honor of the tribal segment. Alienating that amount of land, about five hectares, was seen as a way of making the territory of the tribal segment smaller, with fewer resources, and thereby weaker.

Mr. M had his own interests to consider and knew he would not lose honor by joining another larger and richer tribal segment. He fortified his house and sandbagged his windows, and sporadic fighting broke out. Since the conflict developed between territorial units within the tribe (*qabila*) of Anis, the matter was taken before the most influential shaykh in Anis, Bayt Muqdad, who arranged a cease-fire and exerted pressure on the conflicting parties to work toward a settlement. For Mr. M, the issue was getting convenient access to his house, which rested on resolving the road alignment issue. An interesting point was that the resistance to the road did not come from Bani Khalad, but from other members of al-Hada' who opposed the route because it would come too close to the foraging areas used by their women, opening the door for "strangers" to enter their area and threaten the honor of their women.[9]

It is interesting to note that in this case members of Mr. M's own descent group did not come to his aid but, instead, opposed his movement since their primary obligations were with to their tribal segment. Additionally, the Maghrabit al-ʿAnis case is also evidence that territorial integrity is very important in maintaining the corporate nature of tribal groups, a point discussed in more detail in chapter 7.

Attempts to sell land can raise equal problems, as a case in southwestern Anis near the border of ʿUtama indicates.[10] This incident is particularly interesting because it is compounded by some national political factors.

In ʿUtama, the National Democratic Front, locally known as the *jubha*, was interested in gaining political control of the area and began to meddle in local affairs, stirring up the political pot. Tensions reached the boiling point after an incident in the lowland market Suq as-Sabt between members of the tribe of Anis and residents of ʿUtama. The immediate problem stemmed from a family dispute between two brothers-in-law, both from influential families. Mr. A, an important military officer from Anis, bought some land on the other side of the district (and tribal) border in ʿUtama from his brother-in-law Mr. B, who was away in Saudi Arabia at the time. Unfortunately, the agent who sold the land on behalf of its owner did not have authorization to sell the land while he was away. When Mr. B returned, he was outraged that the agent had sold the land to a man from another tribe and demanded its return. When the Anis man refused, partly because he had already made improvements, bulldozing some terraces (tearing up coffee trees in the process) and drilling a well, Mr. B took his uprooted coffee trees to the governorate seat in Dhamar. He was unsuccessful in his attempts to get assistance, so he went to Sanaʿa to the Ministry of Justice.

This proved to be a bad move, because Mr. A's influence was very high, and Mr. B ended up in jail. At this juncture, Mr. A left the country on business and the *jubha* entered the picture by kidnapping members of Mr. A's family and threatening to wage war in the whole area. Mr. B was released from jail, but the *jubha* had already set fire to Mr. A's house. When Mr. A returned to the country, he had little trouble calling upon his Anis tribesmen for support and formed a small militia to attack ʿUtama. Mr. A was able to get the support of the Anis tribesmen by claiming that his honor had been violated, that he had bought the land legally and his house had been desecrated.

Sensing the vulnerability of the position of the ʿUtama man, Mr. A rallied his men and tried to launch a quick attack on what he thought was the much weaker *jubha* force. Official reports had indicated that the *jubha* was a ragtag bunch of dissidents and not a well-organized group. As Mr. A and his fellow Anis tribesmen raced their jeeps along the road to ʿUtama, the *jubha* allowed them to get well into the narrows of Wadi Kharifa before lowering the boom. The Anis tribesmen, led by a high-ranking military man, were so overconfident that they allowed themselves to be lured into a classical trap and were ambushed. Many were killed, and Mr. A barely escaped with his life. The officer returned to get official government support for his position, and the ʿUtama man was stuck with his alliance with the *jubha*. The lines were drawn for a protracted struggle that lasted over a year and a half.

Later on, some of the *jubha* men encountered the Anis tribesmen in the market at Suq as-Sabt, supposedly a "neutral" zone; an argument ensued, and some people were shot. This was the spark that touched off the flames of a local war.

In this case, the man from Anis knew that by purchasing the lands in ʿUtama he would present a challenge to his brother-in-law (with whom he had a personal dispute), but he thought he could get away with it by buying the property while the owner was out of the country. An interesting aspect of this case is that the man from Anis did not initially get much support for his position from his fellow tribesmen. Although he had legally paid for the land and had made improvements, from the perspective of tribal ethics, he had violated a tacit understanding of reciprocal respect for tribal boundaries. The people of Anis having experienced similar challenges, and having reacted with force in defense of their territory, understood the position of the ʿUtama people and held back. The purchase of the land was generally regarded as a legal but sneaky thing to do, not indicative of a high standard of honor and therefore not worthy of much tribal support. Initially, it was a matter between two brothers-in-law that should have been solved locally; but once the violence started, property was destroyed, and women were threatened, the Anis tribesmen quickly rallied to his call for action.

In sum, we may picture Anis as one large tribe that is subdivided into about a dozen major segments and about fifty subsegments. Each segment is a named political identity that is intimately linked to the territory. Superimposed on this tribal structure is a system of state administrative divisions consisting of the *qadaʾ*, the three districts (*nahiyas*) Dawran, Jabal ish-Shirq, and Maʿbar/Jahran, and fifty-seven subdistricts (*ʿuzlas*).[11]

Jibal Rayma

Jibal Rayma presents a significant contrast to Anis. Absent from its social organization is the tribal core. The people of Jibal Rayma do not conceive of their social organization in terms of tribes; the term *qabila* is not used to refer to any political, kinship, or territorial entities. Rather, the organizational landscape of Jibal Rayma is dominated by the state administrative system, itself a revamping of the older imamic structure. Jibal Rayma is a *qadaʾ* composed of five districts — Bilad it-Taʿam, as-Salafiya, al-Jabin, al-Jaʿfariya, and Kusma.

Each district is composed of a number of *ʿuzlas*, and each *ʿuzla* broken down into *mughrams*. The *ʿuzlas* and *mughrams*, like all territorial divisions in Yemen, may have a name that suggests a genealogical basis or they may not. One finds *ʿuzlas* named after mountains, physical features, and people, but there is no significance to place names per se.

The *ʿuzlas* in Jibal Rayma are relatively small, ranging in size from ten to seventy-five square kilometers. The size of the *ʿuzla* is to a large extent determined by the productivity of the land. In the well-watered and fertile higher elevations, where agriculture is more intensive, the population is denser and the *ʿuzlas* are smaller (or subdivided into smaller units). In the rugged lower elevations, the *ʿuzlas* incorporate larger areas. For example, in the arid region southeast of Kusma bordering the upper reaches of Wadi Rimaʿ, the *ʿuzlas* ar-Rim and Bani Yaʿafar each cover about fifty square kilometers, with only about 1,400 residents per *ʿuzla*. Occasionally, large *ʿuzlas* are found in the densely populated highlands, but they are broken down into smaller administrative units called *mughrams*. For example, the *ʿuzla* Bani Tulayli contains the smaller *mughrams* Shaʿaf, Bani Mansur, ʿIyna, and Saluka. Each of these *mughrams* covers about four or five square kilometers and numbers about 1,200 people. If an *ʿuzla* is small, it is isomorphic with the *mughram*.

Each *ʿuzla* is represented by a shaykh, but these are not shaykhs of *tribal* sections. Regardless of the number of *mughrams* in an *ʿuzla*, each *ʿuzla* has only one shaykh (the role of leaders is discussed in more detail later in this chapter). These shaykhs to some extent function like tribal shaykhs in that they are involved in the mediation of local disputes, but in prerevolutionary times they were tied closely with the imam's administrative structure. Thus, their existence is based on different ideological principles.

Completing the complement of local-level leaders is the office of the community secretary (*amin*). Each *mughram* has an *amin* who is directly elected by the important families in the community. The office of *amin* is attached to the director of finance; the *amin* is the local representative of the tax office.

The segmentary lineage system in Jibal Rayma follows the same principles of social group formation as in the general model for all of Yemen; but in Jibal Rayma, the potential size of kin-based action groups is much smaller than in the tribal regions. In each *mughram*

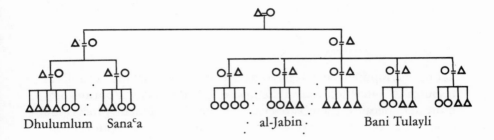

Figure 3. Sample descent group indicating residence, Jibal Rayma

it is possible to find many small descent groups. This is because every family in the area traces its ancestry to some other part of the country; there are no original Jibal Rayma families. Even the oldest of families in Jibal Rayma record a presence of only two or three hundred years. Thus, the descent groups they form are comparatively small. In short, families are scattered across the mountainside in little hamlets. One has cousins located here and there, but there are very few large territories associated with one or two large descent groups (as there are in Anis). This can be seen in an example taken from Kusma, Jibal Rayma. In this descent group, which carried back only four generations, the families were spread over three areas in Jibal Rayma (Bani Tulayli and Jabal Dhulumlum in Kusma *nahiya* and al-Jabin), and one branch of the family had emigrated to Sanaᶜa. The largest concentration of members of this descent group was in one *mahal* near Kusma village, made up of three extended family households.

The social structures of Jibal Rayma and Anis are similar to the extent that both have a segmentary lineage system with the ability to coalesce kinsmen into larger groups when collective action is needed and because of the existence of the state administrative system. However, the social systems in the two areas differ significantly in tribal organization, in relative importance of the state system in regulating public affairs, and in the extent to which kinship ties unite the residents.

POWER AND LOCAL POLITICS

Local development involves collective decision making and local resource mobilization for public investment that benefit entire communities. Because these two facets of the development process are essentially political in nature, an understanding of the political constellations and processes concerned with the generation and disposition of power is important. In Anis and Jibal Rayma, there are a number of similarities as well as some very significant differences in the type of power wielded by local leaders, the distribution of power in the community, its stability over time, and the role of the central government administration in local affairs. To develop the background for an analysis of local development, a comparison of power brokers, how power is obtained and maintained, and where the loci of power are found in each area is necessary. Given that development and change in Yemen became widespread only after the 1962 revolution, it is appropriate to include a recent historical perspective in the discussion of power in the rural areas.

Anis

Anis is, first and foremost, a tribe. Thus, it make sense to begin an analysis of power relations with a discussion of the role of the tribal leaders in the regulation of public affairs. The excellent discussions of the role of shaykhs in the northern tribes by Dresch (1984, 1986) are quite applicable to Anis. Dresch observes that the power of tribal shaykhs does not necessarily derive from control of large tracts of land and the economic advantages so enjoined; nor is it associated with the control of taxes (which were regulated by the imam's agents). Furthermore, the power of the shaykh among his fellow tribal brothers, it has been observed, is not a coercive one; shaykhs do not command standing tribal militia. Rather, the power of tribal shaykhs stems from their role as arbitrators in local affairs. As part of their business, one may think of tribal shaykhs as paralegal professionals who delve into problems involving *ʿuruf*, or tribal law. The more successful the shaykh is at negotiation, the more refined his skills at persuasion (Caton 1987), the larger his clientele. The more cases he has, the greater his power potential. Dresch (1984) describes the process whereby plaintiffs take their problems to the shaykh of their choosing. If a shaykh decides to represent a tribesman (or group), he takes a surety; from that point on, the tribesman is bound through an intricate system of tribal moral codes and, most importantly, by his honor (*sharaf*, *wajh*) to suspend his action. Once the surety is taken, the shaykh has assumed a position of power, and the plaintiff has assumed a subordinate position; the shaykh guarantees the behavior of his client. Successful shaykhs have many cases under consideration at one time and consequently quite a bit of influence.

Shaykhs, especially successful ones, very often have wealth. The debate of whether the power of tribal shaykhs is based on economic leverage and coercive power or on more ideological notions of tribal honor is a bit misleading. They are different forms of power and may exist in tandem. One avenue for accumulating wealth is the profit generated in the paralegal profession. Sometimes the shaykh may take on a case and, seeing that his client is in the right and that he is entitled to compensation, may pay the damages from his own pocket, then try to recover an amount from the shaykh representing the other party; he may recover much more than he paid to his client. Or he may take a percentage of the settlement. Of course, the more cases, the more revenue generated and the better his finanical position. This wealth can be translated into real property (such as land), be used in demonstrations of largess to gain a reputation, buy favor or influence, or be employed in any number of other ways. The main source of the shaykh's power among his fellow tribesmen is rooted in the tribal system itself and its mechanism for regulating its affairs.

In farming communities, the distribution of land is a good indicator of the nature of power. In support of the argument that Anis does not represent a feudal model, where a small elite controls most of the land and monopolizes power, we may take a look at some of the results from a Yemen agriculture survey. In Anis, about three-quarters of the agricultural land is divided into holdings under ten hectares; the average size of a holding is about one and a half hectares. One can interpret this as indicating that a vast majority of the land is in the hands of small farmers. However, there are large land-owners as well. The remaining quarter of the land is held by 2 per-cent of the population (YARG 1981). Therefore, there are larger estates that stand out in the statistical reports, and some of these are associated with some of the tribal shaykhs and other elite families. These estates require some explanation. Most large estates are found in the middle and upper reaches of Wadi Rima^c and Wadi Siham, extending outward from Madinat ish-Shirq.

The estates are primarily in the wadi bottomland and are typi-cally planted in coffee, millet, and tropical fruits such as papaya and banana. The large estates are owned by wealthy families who live in the surrounding mountains, and the lands are worked by share-croppers and hired laborers. The distinctive feature about these estates is that they are the divided remains of what was once a very large estate owned by the Qassimi imams until the end of the nineteenth century. The major town in the area, located at the junction of the two major wadis, is Madinat ish-Shirq. Until the mid-1970s, the town was called Madinat al-^{c}Abid (city of the slaves). Local history holds that the town was created by the Qassimi imams as a residen-tial camp for the low-status laborers who toiled on the imam's estate. With the fall of the Qassimi dynasty, some highland tribesmen were able to get control of large segments of the land. For example, one of the most influential shaykhs of Anis owns large tracts of land in the immediate vicinity of Madinat ish-Shirq. His large, castlelike house is strategically situated high on a foothill overlooking the wadi. In relation to these lowland wadi residents (*masakin*), he is a feudal lord.

But, as mentioned, these wadi lands were historically worked by the low-status state servants. The descendants of these poor, nontribal people, who are still disenfranchised, continue to labor on the lands. Even after the revolution, these poorer, low-status, uneducated work-ers were not in any position to take advantage of the new possibili-ties for improving their social and economic standards. For example, they did not form part of the new wage-earning force that found employment in the neighboring oil-rich countries. For these wadi-dwelling, nontribal laborers, little had changed. By contrast, in the highlands, among the tribesmen (*qaba'il*), few large estates exist and those that do are often sharecropped by small farmers who wish to supplement their earnings.

In Anis, the tenant-landlord relationship must be seen a source of power that occurs in tandem with the power of tribal shaykhs, but this aspect of power applies mostly to the landlords' hold over the low-status wadi-dwelling laborers, not fellow tribesmen. Also, it should be pointed out that some of the large landowners are not shaykhs, so one must not make a facile equation between wealth and tribal leadership.

Another point that must be taken into consideration is that many of the larger holdings in the mountains are located in the high plains areas not associated with intensive cultivation. The yields from the nonirrigated, relatively dry, and windswept regions near Maᶜbar/ Jahran or the lower semiproductive wadi slopes near Qaᶜ al-Haql are much smaller than the fertile protected valleys like Qaᶜ Bakil, and the rainswept terraces of Jabal ish-Shirq, so the size of the holdings tends to be larger.

My general impression of Anis is a combination of a feudal structure where large landowners hold power over the poor (*masakin*) of the wadis, and, in the highlands among the tribesmen, a structure of relative equality in landowning and agriculture; my observations of tribal shaykhs indicate that most do not have that much power over fellow tribesmen based on inequitable distribution of highland property. Among fellow Anis tribesmen, the larger landowners have little coercive power or leverage apart from what money can buy; agriculture is no longer the only road to riches.

After the revolution, and as a consequence of the regional economic boom in the neighboring oil-producing countries, considerable economic change occurred. More people gained wealth, and a new class of professionals, people with education or experience in the military, migrant workers, businessmen, doctors, and the like began to emerge. But these professionals were, for the most part, men from the tribe, symbolic brothers of the shaykhs with quite similar interests—making money and bettering the quality of life. The position of the shaykhs of Anis vis-à-vis this new class was not one of a feudal patron-client relationship, but, rather, consensually generated leadership maintained through a shared tribal ideology. Thus, there was not much basis for conflict of interests.

Also, the power of the shaykhs did not emanate from any direct position within the imam's system and thus was not lost with the advent of the revolution. In other words, the revolution did not create a power vacuum in Anis. The shaykhs and elites continued their business as leaders in the regulation of public affairs within the tribe; after the revolution, the people continued to take their problems to their shaykhs. For example, on my visits to the *mudir*'s office in the *qada'* center Dawran I found it surprisingly devoid of activity at four in the afternoon, which is the prime time set aside for qat chewing and conducting the business of rural civil administration. I found little evidence that tribesmen were shifting from the use of their tribal shaykhs to the nontribal state legal/administrative system as a vehicle for settling conflicts. A shift of power in the regulation of local affairs to the postrevolutionary government administrative system was not apparent.

The basic structure of power within the tribe was not radically changed by the revolution or the economic growth that followed. Shaykhs were equally free to take advantage of the new economic opportunities along with the other tribesmen, and many did. Others were content to stay within their customary roles. Thus, the conflict and competition between the shaykhs and elites and the emerging class of newly educated (who are sometimes called the *shabab*) were not heightened to any extent by the revolution or the economic changes that followed. The traditional business of the tribal shaykhs remained intact.

New business was also emerging in the form of the local development association, the brainchild of the *shabab*. As we shall see later in our discussion, this development association was also situated in the public domain and associated with power—the power to allocate and distribute public funds—but this was a *new* order of business, one not previously controlled to any extent by the tribal leaders. Thus, it did not necessarily challenge the power base of the old order. But first, this picture of power in Anis is contrasted with the situation in Jibal Rayma.

Jibal Rayma

In Jibal Rayma, there are some similarities, but more significant differences in stability of the power structures. As noted in the beginning of the chapter, Jibal Rayma is organized according to administrative district, *not* tribal territories. These ʿuzlas date back to before the revolution and were a part of the imam's administrative system. Furthermore, it was pointed out that the ʿuzla were essentially administrative divisions drawn up for the management of tax assessment, accounting, and collection. During the prerevolutionary period, local political power in Jibal Rayma was held by two categories of people, the *sayyids* (descendants of the Prophet Muhammad) and the local shaykhs, both of whom were closely tied to the imam's administrative system. The local *sayyids*, who still own some of the largest and oldest houses in Kusma, controlled relatively large tracts of land. For example, in Kusma district, one of the prime coffee-producing areas is near the perennial stream in Wadi as-Sayyid, along a two-kilometer stretch where the altitude ranges from 840 to 1,000 meters. The name itself is an indication that, prior to the revolution and the economic changes that followed, one important family of *sayyids* owned most of this rich coffee-producing area. This is a relatively level stretch of wadi, quite sheltered, where gravity-flow irrigation is possible through a small system of channels. On each side of this wadi, an area two kilometers long and about forty terraces high can be watered. This particular tract is almost all coffee, being at too low an altitude to grow good qat. Of course, in prerevolutionary times coffee was the main cash crop in the region. In fact, the importance of coffee, as well as qat, has a very long history in the area (Kennedy 1987:71); the eighteenth-century Danish explorer Carsten Niebuhr (1792) refers to Jibal Rayma as "the coffee mountain."

Likewise, the *sayyids* who live in the Kusma district center were important during the prerevolutionary period. They were involved in management of the *waqf* (religious endowment) properties and the collection of *zakat* and were the court judges and, of course, the spokesmen for the imam. Before the revolution, the Kusma *sayyids* used to call all of the merchants and nearby residents together in their relatively large courtyards to read the proclamations of the imam to the people and report the official news of the government.

The second category of power brokers in the prerevolutionary structure were the local shaykhs. In Jibal Rayma, these shaykhs, it must be emphasized, were not tribal. Rather, they were more closely tied to the imam's administrative structure. As one local shaykh described the situation, each ʿ*uzla* had a shaykh who was charged with the task of overseeing local affairs, solving disputes at a local level (for which he received a settlement fee), and supervising tax collection, for which he received up to 10 percent. These shaykhs were in a position to enhance their economic power by virtue of their connections to the state bureaucracy. However, the immediate power base, as determined by their direct access to tax revenues, was limited to their particular *ᶜuzla*, so their territory was in effect limited, as was their potential strength. In Jibal Rayma, the situation that prevailed up until the revolution was a system of many petty shaykhs who derived power from the economic productivity of relatively small territories.

Of course, the system of shaykhs had to have a method of dealing with problems above the *ᶜuzla* level; and in Jibal Rayma, there was a hierarchical structure. In each district, one of the *ᶜuzla* shaykhs, generally the one with the best negotiating skills, would mediate problems at the *ᶜuzla* level; if problems crossed district boundaries, there was a generally recognized paramount shaykh (*shaykh al-masha'ikh*) who could be called on to mediate problems that involved a number of shaykhs. Again, the paramount shaykh himself was only an *ᶜuzla* shaykh, with direct access only to his *ᶜuzla* tax base; but as mediator of larger disputes, he was in a position further to enhance his financial position and therefore his power. It should be noted that in the past hundred years this office shifted three times; the most recent paramount shaykh, who is from near al-Jabin, has only held this office since the revolution.[12] It had previously been held by a shaykh in the Masbahi *ᶜuzla* in the south-central Kusma district; immediately after the expulsion of the Turks following World War I, Qasim al-Mahjar, who lived near Kusma district, tried to form his own ministate within the kingdom.

To get an idea of the economic position of a typical shaykh's family, we may look at the case of one of the more important families in Kusma. The estimated total area of the *mughram* Shaᶜaf is four square kilometers (400 hectares), with a population of 140 families. If all the land were shared equally, this would yield approximately 2.8 hectares per family, slightly above the national average. The largest landowner in the area was the shaykh's family, which held about 20 hectares or roughly 5 percent of the land. Members of this family had come to the area some 150 years ago from the Hashid region, most probably as agents of the imam, and had settled in a rich agricultural area. As *ᶜuzla* shaykhs, they were entitled to retain about 10 percent of the *zakat* and used this wealth to acquire prime land. Most of this land was planted in qat (although there were also some coffee plots), and the family employed occasional laborers to weed and work in the fields and had a crew of about seven porter/middlemen who picked the crop, wrapped it, transported it to the regional markets, and retailed it. This land generated considerable income for the family, which also had a few families of sharecroppers working some of the land in cereal production.[13]

So in Jibal Rayma, prior to the revolution, there was a class of larger landowners, made up mostly of shaykhs and *sayyids*, who held most political and economic power. It must be pointed out that the scale of their power was limited: they did not have masses of tenants as in other areas in the western highlands.[14] Most of the farmers in Sha'af, and in Jibal Rayma as a whole, owned their own house and worked their own property, supplementing it with sharecropping agreements. The shaykhs were dependent on the additional labor provided on a contractual basis by small farmers to work their lands. But the small farmers also had enough property to make a living on their own. The economic power base of the local shaykhs in Jibal Rayma was, therefore, comparatively small; their advantage, while significant, was not as out of proportion as in other areas.

There were, and still are, some large landowners, but most of the land is in small holdings; so it is stretching the data to argue that they formed a landowning class with so much financial leverage as to have a coercive hold over sizable populations. In Jibal Rayma, there are a number of shaykhs with limited influence over relatively small, atomistic areas. Their relative wealth puts them in an advantageous position to exert their political will.

With the advent of the revolution and the new economic opportunities brought about by the high rate of emigration, shifts in wealth and power began to occur in the area. First of all, the old linkages between the shaykhs and *sayyids* and the government were broken, and there was competition to fill the newly created government administrative offices. The revolution stripped away quite a bit of their power and financial resources. For example, the shaykhs were no longer tied directly to the tax collection and the large percentage of the take. Instead, tax collection was turned over to the *mughram* secretary, the *amin*. His entitlement was much less, on the order of 1 to 3 percent. Some of the shaykhs or members of the shaykh families succeeded in making the transition and moved into new government roles, but others did not. For example, the brother of the paramount shaykh in al-Jabin became director of security for the entire region, thus keeping a good deal of political power in the family. The brother of another shaykh became the *amin* of a nearby subdistrict. In a third case, a member of the *sayyid* family of Kusma became assistant *hakim* (judge), another became assistant district director, and another the secretary to the district director. However, many other shaykhs and elites were excluded from the new order. The revolution did succeed in change, and some of the local offices were occupied by people not formerly associated with the prerevolutionary power brokers. For example, in Sha°af the office of *amin* went to a respected elder of the community, not to a shaykh. In Kusma, the office of the director of the municipality went to a merchant who had only few small landholdings.

Another significant change was that the power associated with the wealth differentials between the elites and the average tribesmen derived from agriculture was to some extent diminished by the changes in the regional economy. Many new possibilities for increasing personal wealth were created by emigration. Small farmers, many of whom used to have labor contracts with the larger coffee plantation owners (to bring in supplemental cash necessary to maintain the farm), began to emigrate to Saudi Arabia, where they were better paid and could amass a small fortune in savings. Their remitted earnings allowed for a construction boom and increased opportunities in trade and business. More and more people were acquiring a higher degree of personal affluence, and some merchants became quite wealthy. As noted in chapter 4, the competition for labor by Saudi Arabia also caused general inflation, especially in wages.

For those larger landowners whose fortunes were tied to coffee, and therefore to the vicissitudes of a commodity market, the rising labor costs reduced the profit margins on the crop, and it became increasingly difficult to get laborers. Furthermore, the international demand for Yemeni coffee dropped because of the high degree of local variation in the quality of the crops and the difficulties in grading the product.[15] The financial fortunes of those tied to coffee production in Jibal Rayma began to be significantly reduced. While it still is a profitable crop, relative to the other changes in the economy, it is not nearly as profitable as in the past (Kennedy 1987:158). In short, the economic leverage and the power associated with landownership were weakened as a result of the economic changes in the postrevolutionary period; newly created wealth was challenging the old order.

A third area of change in power involves the degree of involvement of the state administrative system in local affairs. In prerevolutionary times, dispute settlement was the purview of the shaykhs and *sayyids*; but after the revolution, the state administrative and judicial system offered a new alternative. Instead of taking a problem to the shaykh, it was possible to take it to the government-appointed director of the district, the *mudir* of the *nahiya*. In this regard, it must again be remembered that in Jibal Rayma, the shaykhs are not leaders of tribes or tribal sections. There are no tribes, so there is no tribal ideology to support their claims to the role of mediator as there is in the tribal heartland or, for that matter, in Anis. As mentioned in the general discussion of the sources of power, dispute settlement is one of the major power venues throughout Yemen. In Jibal Rayma, the *mudir* became a popular alternative to the shaykh for settling disputes; in some sections of Jibal Rayma, there were significant portions of the population who no longer recognized the title or office of the shaykhs. For example, in Sha°af (after the death of the °*uzla* shaykh about ten years prior to this research), the eldest son's claim to the title was rejected by many of the community members, who stated flatly that there was no longer an office of shaykh in the °*uzla*, only the elected *mughram amin*s. However, in villages more remote from his immediate village, the shaykh's claim is more recognized.

The *mudir* was one alternative to the shaykh as arbitrator; successful businessmen and educated professionals were newer ones. In cases where people did not want to take a problem to the *mudir*, either because he did not have a good reputation for fairness or because they feared that getting tangled in the state legal system might prove too costly and time-consuming, many began to seek out people who had solid reputations for judgement (°*aql*) and/or the economic ability to take on a case and "prepay" the settlement. These individuals, some of whom were successful merchants from rather ignoble family backgrounds, emerged as new power brokers, stealing even more of the business of the shaykhs.

As a result of the rush to fill the power vacuum created by the revolution, the present picture of power in Jibal Rayma is one of a nontribal area fragmented between a weakened class of shaykhs and *sayyids*, a new class of professionals and educated leaders, some wealthy businessmen, and a host of small farmers with increased experience and political awareness who are expressing their views—what might be characterized as an emerging middle class.

As an example of the kinds of tensions and attempts to gain power in the changing system, we can look at one futile effort by a shaykh who was steadily losing power. As I have argued, the advantageous position during the imam's period resulted in some shaykhs amassing significant wealth. In the postrevolutionary shuffle (still underway), some have attempted to use their wealth to buy more influence to replace the power already lost. One especially viable target for these political machinations can be found among those civil authorities vulnerable to bribes. For example, a shaykh from a community just east of the Kusma center tried to bribe the director of security of the area to let him have his own contingent of armed police. He succeeded in having soldiers assigned to his house, but he was confronted one evening by a group of educated young men, and his attempt at grabbing a little more power was thwarted. (This story is more fully detailed later in the book because it involved the LDA as well.) The shaykh was overstepping his bounds, so he was immediately confronted, a scuffle broke out, and he was eventually forced to return the soldiers.

SUMMARY

The changes prompted by the revolution and following economic growth affected the power structures in the two areas differently. In Anis, where the economic power of the elites was tied to private ownership of some large estates worked by low-status (nontribal), disenfranchised laborers and sharecroppers, the revolution had little effect; private property was not confiscated or redistributed. Furthermore, the people who worked these lands were so far down the social ladder that they were in no position to take advantage of the new opportunities arising from emigration. They remained tied to the land, working for the landlords, and were not a part of the labor pool of potential emigrants whose wages were inflating. Second, the tribal shaykhs and elites held their position among the tribesmen by virtue of a consensus and an ideology of tribal equality. In general, the tribesmen of Anis were not in any serious economic dependency relationship to the elites. The shaykhs and other leaders (*sayyids*, *qadhis*, etc.) continued in their role as local mediators outside the state judicial system. Since the new class of educated professionals came from the tribesmen themselves, they did not pose a direct threat to the power domains traditionally held by the elites. With this background of local political continuity and economic change, the stage was set for the emergence of the local development associations as a new locus of power, but one that would not directly pose a challenge to the old order.

In contrast, in Jibal Rayma there were the following shifts in power following the revolution: (1) the shaykhs lost their right to the tax base and their linkages to the power of the *ancient régime* were severed; (2) the economic gap between the shaykhs and other elites and the average person was narrowed; and (3) the role of the shaykhs and *sayyids* as mediators, to a large extent, was usurped by the *mudir* and other new brokers. A power vacuum was created by the revolution. In the prerevolutionary system power derived from the relationship of leaders to the imam's administrative system — that is, it originated from above rather than being based on local consensus or supported by any popular ideology. In this postrevolutionary period, the new power relations in Jibal Rayma are still being defined and the local development associations that emerged in the 1970s have been caught up to one degree or another in this political shuffling.

The following chapters explore how the functioning of the LDAs in Anis and Jibal Rayma has been affected by these differences in social organization and power.

6

Local Politics, Corporate Groups, and Development

One of the key elements in local rural development in Yemen is the ability of the people to act in a corporate manner. Local development involves the utilization of public resources for public benefit and requires considerable cooperation and coordination of effort. Financial resources must be drawn from the public in the form of tax revenues and direct contributions, decisions must be taken on which areas are to be allocated a project, and type of projects must be agreed upon. Outside funding sources and approvals must be obtained, which often requires intense lobbying efforts. Contracts must be tendered, problems in logistics solved, and so forth. In rural Yemen, local development activities are intricately interwoven with the local and regional political organization. Any group trying to implement a development project, whether it is a formal local development association or an ad hoc delegation of community leaders, must have the ability to act in a corporate manner in order to accomplish anything. Therefore, in order to examine the process of local development in Jibal Rayma and Anis, corporate group functioning and underlying sociopolitical similarities and differences need to be taken into account. In this chapter, the analysis of Yemen sociopolitical organization and local development is taken a step further through a structured comparison of rural organization in the western central highlands.

CORPORATE GROUPS AND LOCAL DEVELOPMENT

M. G. Smith's ideas on traditional sociopolitical organization are a useful starting point for analysis of local development because he provides an expanded concept of corporate groups that allows for

121

cross-cultural comparison. According to Smith's formulation, a corporate group is "an enduring body or polity that has organizational structure, defined membership and identity" (1974:176–97). In order for a political unit to be considered a corporate group, it must have the structure and organization required to regulate public affairs. Using this definition, it may be argued that the tribe (*qabila*), the minimal agnatic unit (*bayt*), and the administrative divisions of the *qada'*, *nahiya*, and perhaps the *'uzla* (see chapter 3) are corporate groups that form the local sociopolitical environment. The local development associations, by definition, are also corporate groups. In contrast to corporate groups, Smith (1974) defines political entities without the capacity for control and regulation of public affairs as corporate categories. In the western central highlands of Yemen, the main corporate categories include the social-hierarchical divisions (such as *sayyid*s and tribesmen [*qaba'il*]), other status categories (e.g., *bani khums* and *akhdam*), and the major religious sects.

The Tribe as a Corporate Group

There is considerable debate on whether or not the tribe can be considered a corporate group. Dresch, for example, is adamant that tribes are not corporate entities: "They [the tribes] have no corporate life — no standing economic or political structure — which would allow one to define them, as it were, from within" (1984:35). However, it may be argued that Dresch is taking a very narrow view of what constitutes a corporate group. While it is true that there is no explicit organizational structure on the model of Western businesses, and no tribal businesses such as one finds, for example, among contemporary American Indian tribes, Yemeni tribes do have an incipient structure most often noted when the tribes come together in times of stress. Therefore, there are reasons for considering the tribes in the western central highlands of Yemen to be corporate groups, especially when including the other defining features of the model outlined by Smith (1974).

The tribe clearly has a determinate membership, an incipient organization, endurance over time, and the ability to control public affairs. In Yemen, the tribe may trace its heritage and history over many hundreds of years, and it is usually rooted in some mythical origin in the earliest history of Yemen. As seen in chapter 6, it contains specific offices (i.e., *masha'ikh*) and has an informal administrative structure. The tribe is a specifically delineated unit, with both social and geographical boundaries, and a determinate membership based to some extent on both kinship and residence.[1] As for the means of regulating public affairs and exerting order and control over its membership, customary or tribal law (*ʿuruf*) and the moral ethos (*qabayla*) set clear standards for behavior, provide the guidelines for socially acceptable action, and stipulate the sanctions and means of retribution in case of violation (Adra 1982). Mediation of most disputes is accomplished within the tribal organization. The tribe also has the ability on special occasions to function as a whole, as the example of unity in recent wars demonstrates.

Within the kin-based structure, the intermediate levels of organization (the lineage-based groups— *habl, fakhdh, lahma,* and the like) also carry the potential to coalesce into corporate groups, but rarely do so. They are more a "social organization in reserve" (Adra 1982; Meeker 1979) that can mobilize under certain circumstances requiring collective action, such as blood feud, the need to collect blood money (*diya*), or times of economic stress. However, adhering to Smith's model, these larger kin-based groups have no offices, titles, or administrative structures that endure over time. In these groups, the genealogical criteria can be shifted to expand or restrict the size of the group, depending on the circumstances (e.g., number of generations). Therefore, they only occasionally form corporate groups.

At the local level, corporate groups again emerge in the form of minimal agnatic units, including the *da'ima*, the *bayt*, and the *ʿusra*. They are economic units, with a patriarchal structure, clearly delineated in terms of membership (three or four generations), enduring over time, and with internal means for controlling and regulating their affairs. In the tribal household, the senior male is nominally the head of the household and remains so, symbolically at least, until his death. Of course, management of the unit transfers to the sons with advancing age.

A household may consist of a number of nuclear families, so each head of a nuclear family is responsible for his own family affairs. With the natural expansion of the extended family, new minimal agnatic units are created over time through a process of social fission. Residency tends to be patrilocal or neolocal. Upon marriage, daughters shift to their husband's households. This often involves the transfer of the wife's personal property and inheritance. In the case of a number of brothers inhabiting the same household, a typical pattern is for the eldest to assume the position of head of the household, but there is no hard and fast rule of primogeniture. Typically, each head of a nuclear family handles his own affairs, while responsibility for management of the entire extended family unit is obtained through consensus. However, if need arises for a general spokesman or leader of the unit, it is customary for either the oldest male or the one with the most reason (*ʿaql*) to assume such a position.

The kinds of collective action that a household typically engages in revolve around maintaining the family farm and sharing costs for house repair, construction, and improvements and, of course, responsibility in case of loss of family honor, blood feuds, or intratribal conflicts. Combined effort for maintaining the extended household farm is not insignificant. Islamic inheritance laws provide for an equal share among sons, and each daughter is entitled to one-half of a brother's share. Consequently, before the death of the father, the land holdings are legally divided, and each brother could elect to farm only his segment by himself. In practice, this does not often occur; greater benefit is derived through common operation, which frees some of the males to engage in other income-producing activities. All in all, the household functions as one economic unit, though each nuclear family often controls its own financial and personal affairs.

Nontribal Corporate Groups

Nontribal or territorial corporate groups must be understood in the context of the history of their development in Yemen. The *nahiya*, *qada'*, and *ʿuzla* are classified as nontribal because they are divisions of an administrative system based on territorial considerations and not on the genealogical/kinship idiom. They are government entities with specified boundaries, membership determined by residence, and a specific set of administrative offices. As mentioned in chapter 4, the *nahiya*, for example, contains the offices of *mudir* (director), *mudir al-mal* (financial director), *hakim* (judge), and the heads of various service departments. As basic units in the administrative system, the offices in this structure regulate public activities, among others, the areas of taxation, education, public security, and health.

Of course, the local development association also meets the requirements for a corporate group according to Smith's (1974) definition.

The LDA is now a permanent feature on the rural political scene. However, it is more an organization designed to use local resources to address the needs of the community than an extension of the state administrative system. Membership is determined by residence in an incorporated area and leadership is provided by community members elected to its various offices; regulation of affairs is conducted under basic rules and guidelines formulated by the national charter and the Confederation of Yemen Development Associations.

The successful functioning of the LDA as a corporate group is a very important factor in assessing the process of local rural development. The LDA, as the most recent type of corporate group in Yemen, is evolving and functioning within both the traditional local political system and the state bureaucracy. Therefore, it is important to examine the structure and functioning of the LDAs in the two *qada*'s of Jibal Rayma and Anis within the overall sociopolitical context, including the traditional system.

Tiffany (1979), expanding on the corporate analysis model of Smith (1974), has suggested a framework for organizing analyses of political systems. It is useful because the model is designed to "contribute to the development of cross-cultural studies and systems analysis by providing units that (1) are precisely defined, (2) are directly comparable and (3) are critical for governing regularities of political structure and change" (Tiffany 1979:74). It is also well suited for intracultural controlled comparisons since it highlights salient differences between political units. Tiffany's model incorporates nine factors — perpetuity, recruitment principles, a determinate membership, identity, common affairs, internal and external organization, procedures for conducting unit affairs, and autonomy. Using these nine principles as a guideline for comparing the political organization of Jibal Rayma and Anis, the significant differences between the two *qada*'s in terms of their ability to function in a corporate fashion to further local development can be explored.

LOCAL POLITICAL ORGANIZATION

Anis

Anis is both a subprovince (*qada'*) in the state administrative system and a tribe (*qabila*) in the traditional social system. It has periodically been of importance in Yemeni history. The historian Hassan ibn Ahmad al-Hamdani, writing in the tenth century A.D., makes repeated reference to the tribe and some of the great castles of Anis (Lofgren 1953). In the generally accepted local version of the Anis tribal genealogy, a historical figure named Anis is one of the descendants of Bakil. Thus, the Anis tribesmen consider themselves members of the Bakil federation. At the opening of the seventeenth century, the town of Dawran Anis, built under the shadow of the ancient ruin of Damigh, was the seat of the Zaydi Qassimi Imamate. Local history is full of accounts of military campaigns launched against the Turks during both the first (seventeenth-century) and second (nineteenth-century) occupations. As a tribe, Anis continues to maintain its integrity in the changing sociopolitical environment.

Internal migration into the region is low, so membership in the tribe is determined primarily by birth. Political organization in Anis entails both the traditional tribal segmentary system and the overlapping state administrative organization. The set of divisions most important in daily affairs is based more on territorial and political concerns than on kinship. In Anis, there is a strong correlation among the tribal segments, the administrative divisions, and the large descent groups (*fakhdh*s) that form the backbone of the local political organization.

While tribal leadership in Anis is vested in the offices of the *masha'ikh*, after the revolution there was some degree of disaffection among the younger professionals and intellectuals, but this discord was not very intense and the competition for many of the newly created government offices was open. With the expansion of the civil administration, the importance of the *masha'ikh* has declined, but is by no means in eclipse; they still serve an important function in adjudicating local disputes. Thus, the traditional leadership in Anis has not been static and entrenched in the old tradition, but dynamic and adaptable. Since the revolution, there have been strong political ties between Anis and the central government. Several prominent political figures in the republic's administration in both the executive and military branches are from Anis, and these ties add to the tribe's strength and ability to lobby for government assistance. At the level of governorate politics, Anis is the most populated and powerful tribe in Dhamar. Also, as an almost entirely Zaydi tribe, Anis is part of the sectarian majority in the governorate.

From antiquity, tribes such as Anis have maintained the autonomy to conduct their own affairs without excessive control by any centralized authority or outside influence, and this continues today. For example, in 1981, when the National Democratic Front was active in nearby regions in Dhamar governorate, it was not able to make inroads into Anis. One informant explained this by contrasting Anis with other areas. He described Anis as stable, firmly set in its political position, and united as a traditional political unit. In contrast, he characterized the neighboring districts (ʿUtama, Wasab as-Safil, and Wasab al-ʿAli) as labile, that is, apt to vacillate in response to local political pressure and easily disintegrated because they lacked the strength and unity provided by the institution of the tribe.

The concept of *ʿayana* (help or assistance) is a central element in the relationship between segments of the tribe. Traditionally, it was the duty of any community within the tribe to provide assistance in the event of any natural or human disaster, as well as to aid public projects, such as path construction and building of mosques. Similarly, the duty to provide safe passage and security for travelers was also the collective responsibility of the tribe. Sanctions against any infringement upon an escorted person (*muraffiq*) are much more severe than for a resident. The blood price (*diya*) for a person killed while under the protection of a tribe is eleven times the normal amount, which, if the culprit goes undetected, must be paid by the tribe.

In prerevolutionary times, the main track from the port of al-Hudayda to the capital Sanaʿa passed directly through Anis. This route seems to be ancient — al-Hamdani remarks that the fortresses at Damigh and Masnaʿa overlooked the trail (Faris 1938:42). Historically, the tribe had the responsibility for protecting the traffic that passed through the region.

Prior to the influx of wealth caused by emigration, security throughout Yemen was more unstable, due in large part to frequent raiding of fields in times of sporadic crop failures. Collective responsibility to protect their interests fell on the tribesmen, and organized tribal institutions were necessary to ensure that disputes were settled according to customary law. In modern times, internecine tribal feuding and the frequent need to bring the tribe together as a fighting unit have passed. Threats from other tribes are now mostly a fading memory, but one still fresh enough in the minds of the older generations to assure that the tribe maintains its image of solidarity and strength. An example of this necessity to maintain tribal ethics occurred late in my research when a *muraffiq* was killed by mistake.

A team of engineers was traveling through western Anis, in the lower regions of Jabal ish-Shirq. The engineers (mostly expatriates) had employed the services of an interpreter who was from the Ibb region. Because they were on an official mission for the Ministry of Public Works to evaluate some potential well sites, they were under the care and responsibility of the tribe of Anis. Unfortunately, they were traveling in an out-of-the-way region where few cars passed, and their vehicle resembled one owned by an Anis tribesman who was involved in a personal dispute. A young man, reported to be mentally retarded, had been told by his uncle to kill his adversary, but instead he shot at the engineers' vehicle, killing the translator. The mentally retarded young man was easily located and readily admitted to the shooting, saying that his uncle had told him to do it. He was swiftly tried and executed, and the uncle was sent to prison. In this case, there was sentiment on behalf of the Anis tribesmen that some leniency should be shown to the mentally retarded young man, in that he was not fully aware of what he was doing, but it was decided that an execution was necessary in order to demonstrate that Anis was still a strong tribe capable of guaranteeing the safety of those under its protection. Additionally, it was feared that reprisal from the victim's kin from the Ibb region might cause the problem to escalate, which would be an undesirable consequence from a tragic mistake. The execution of the killer of the engineer was symbolic of the fact that the tribe of Anis still regarded the principle of protection, one of the core tribal values, quite seriously.

From antiquity, the tribe of Anis has maintained the autonomy to conduct its own affairs without excessive control by any centralized authority. Even during the Ottoman occupations of Yemen, there was never much effective control of the rural areas. As evidence of this, the Ottoman administration elected to utilize tribal boundaries in creating its own administrative divisions. "Fiercely independent" is a term that has frequently been used to describe the tribes of Yemen, and this certainly applies to the tribe of Anis. Although it has moderated its position in recent years and no longer maintains active militias, as do some of the northern tribes, it still maintains strong tribal autonomy.

Autonomy is rooted in the very nature of Anis society. At no time in history was Anis dominated by another tribe or faction, and this tradition of autonomy has been carried through in postrevolutionary Yemen. A proverb used in Anis, *ma lahiya yikhdum lahiya* (a bearded man will not serve a bearded man), reflects the people's self-perception that they are equal to the other Yemeni tribes.

Jibal Rayma

Qada' Jibal Rayma is tribal only in the sense that most of the residents of the area claim a noble tribal (*qabili*) heritage. However, Jibal Rayma does not constitute a true tribe. In fact, after repeated investigation, I conclude that there are *no* tribes in Jibal Rayma. Lower-level kin-based groups (extended families and patrilineal descent groups) are the basic social units, but these are not united at any higher level.

According to a local historian, in antiquity Jibal Rayma was a large principality under the suzerainty of the Himyarite prince Ka'ib Wakil Jublan ibn Sahil and was known as Jublan.[2] During this period, Jibal Rayma was on the periphery of the Himyaritic civilization, an agricultural hinterland that had little political or strategic importance. Legend attributes the construction of large ancient houses alleged to have existed in Jibal Rayma to the *jinn* (Faris 1938:21), an obscure reference that indicates a peripheral historical importance. There is, as yet, no archaeological evidence to indicate any cultural florescence in the region.

During the Ottoman occupation, a few garrisons were constructed on the mountain ridges overlooking the Tihama, and al-Jabin was made the administrative center for the region. Taxes were extracted, mostly on coffee production, and the area was peaceful and easily controlled. After the expulsion of the Ottomans at the conclusion of World War I, Jibal Rayma briefly toyed with the idea of becoming an autonomous region. Under the leadership of Qasim al-Mahjar, the people of Jibal Rayma living near Kusma declared they were not under the authority of the imam; but, after a few years, troops were sent in to control the localized rebellion.

Jibal Rayma is different from many of the other regions in Yemen in that most of the residents trace their tribal roots to other areas and claim to have inhabited the region for only a few hundred years. There are numerous gaps in local history and even the tombs of local saints in this Shafiᶜi region are unidentified. The evidence indicates that the present-day people are migrants from other regions of Yemen who, because of their different origins, have not grown into large descent groups.

As we saw in chapter 5, Jibal Rayma is organized along somewhat different administrative divisions than other parts of Yemen. For example, each ᶜ*uzla* in Jibal Rayma is further subdivided into *mughram*s represented by an *amin*. The *mughram* is an interesting unit: the word is derived from the Arabic root *gh-r-m*, which implies collective liability. This is significant because the corporate aspects of the tribe are most clearly seen in times of crisis, and "the test *par excellence* of corporate affiliations is the acceptance of the responsibility to pay blood money" (Peters 1959:47). In Yemeni tribal society, liability is often attached to the descent group; but in Jibal Rayma, the people within the *mughram* did *not* automatically assume a shared liability, which indicates little sense of traditional corporate unity.

Traditional leadership in Jibal Rayma only mimics the tribal model. The offices exist without the formal institution of the tribe and the functions of the *masha'ikh* are being taken over by the *mudir* of the *nahiya*. The traditional position of paramount shaykh has for all practical purposes now become a government office. In its relations with the larger sociopolitical system, Jibal Rayma does not occupy a position of strength or power. At the level of intertribal politics, Jibal Rayma is not an active member of the major Yemeni federations. Some residents of Jibal Rayma are of the opinion that they are more or less aligned with the Bakil federation, but this position is denied by most. Historically, Jibal Rayma may have been a member of the defunct Mathij confederation, but even this is uncertain. Jibal Rayma is on the periphery of the tribal federation system, and the area has not, in recent history, been of much political significance.

In the early 1970s in Jibal Rayma, the issue of the *qada'*s continued association with Sanaᶜa governorate was again raised. Historically, Jibal Rayma had strong political links with al-Hudayda governorate that resulted from its close proximity and economic ties to the main seaport, al-Hudayda. A possible governorate shift was opposed by some of the residents of Jibal Rayma and supported by others. The changes led to armed conflict among the local factions, and the situation required a great deal of negotiation before it was settled.

Part of the problem was that Sana'a was a Zaydi-controlled governorate; Jibal Rayma, a Shafi'i region, was included among the other minority areas in the governorate (e.g., the Isma'ili of Haraz) and was thus at a serious disadvantage in the arena of governorate politics. Al-Hudayda governorate, by contrast, is Shafi'i, and some of the Jibal Rayma residents felt that an administrative association with al-Hudayda would place them in a position to increase their regional political power. However, any realignment would result in local shifts in power, so there was conflict over the issue that eventually required central government intercession to resolve.

Finally, another example of political factionalism above the level of local interests can be seen in the response to the National Democratic Front, which made significant inroads into the region during the period 1981–82, severely disrupting the security of the entire *qada'*. The front correctly considered the people of Jibal Rayma a weak and divided group that would not band together to offer serious resistance to the movement. The threat of impending violence prompted many of the male residents of Jibal Rayma to flee to the capital or to work in Saudi Arabia until the trouble subsided.

In Jibal Rayma, there is an absence of genealogical depth required for the emergence of a traditional corporate identity. The people consider themselves tribal (*qabili*) in that they can trace their ancestry to some of the famous tribes in Yemen, but they do not form a tribe themselves. Since the basis of a tribe is political unity based on identity with an ancient symbol and the people of Jibal Rayma have none, it has been impossible for them to act as a unified tribe would. The histories of the families in Jibal Rayma are relatively short, and there has not been sufficient time for the necessary expansion of the descent groups— through natural growth, attrition, or intermarriage to reach the stage where territorial units and kin groups correspond to each other.

The hamlets and villages in Jibal Rayma are much more atomistic than those of the traditional tribal strongholds of Yemen and areas united through both kinship and territory are much smaller in size. Instead of finding *'uzla*s composed of a few large descent groups, one finds many descent groups with small core memberships. Thus, in Jibal Rayma there is little possibility for widespread unification of the region through the genealogical idiom, real or fictional. Consequently, the potential for solidarity based on putative kinship ties is

Table 13. Local Sociopolitical Situations, Anis and Jibal Rayma

Anis	*Jibal Rayma*
Presumptive Perpetuity	
Historical depth.	Shallow history.
Recruitment	
Birth.	Birth, migration.
Determinant Membership (in order of importance)	
Genealogical idiom, residence.	Residence, lesser emphasis on the genealogical idiom.
Identity	
Tribal, *with* the institution of the tribe.	Tribal, *without* the institution of the tribe.
Common Affairs	
Local development, common defense, maintenance of tribal honor, regulation of tribal affairs.	Local development, weak ethic of common defense.
Internal Organization	
Tribal, putative common ancestry, secondary civil, state administrative.	Civil administrative divisions, nontribal, diverse ancestry, atomistic local communities.
External Organization	
Alliance with tribal federations (Bakil), part of sectarian majority in governorate, strong ties to military, prominent national leaders.	No tribal alliances, part of the sectarian minority in the governorate, nominal ties to military, no national leaders.
Procedures	
Common, tribal law (*ᶜuruf*), shaykhs, tribal ethics (*qabayla*), state court system (Shariᶜa).	State system (*mudir* and courts), new mediators, less regard for shaykhs.
Autonomy	
Strong tribal authority, under central government control.	Under central government control, no tribal autonomy.

absent. Instead, the *qada'* is made up of social units that are motivated primarily to work toward the short-term benefit of their immediate locality.

In the preceding descriptions, the sociopolitical environments of
both Jibal Rayma and Anis were outlined and fundamental differences in social organization emerged. Table 13 summarizes the differences between Jibal Rayma and Anis as outlined by Tiffany's (1979)
nine principles for comparing sociopolitical organizations.

A distinguishing feature of the traditional sociopolitical environment between Jibal Rayma and Anis is the formal institution of the
tribe. In Anis, the tribe is still recognized as an important social
institution; even though the importance of the civil (state) administrative system is growing, the tribe is still a source of group identity
and remains a valid vehicle for organizing cooperative action and
uniting scattered mountain communities for common cause. This
becomes more evident when the most recent corporate groups, the
local development associations, are examined more fully.

Jibal Rayma, in contrast, has never developed a formal tribal
organization. In its traditional administrative organization, Jibal Rayma
had superficial resemblances to the tribal model with offices of
masha'ikh and the like, but it lacks the key ingredients—common
ancestry, a generalized sense of kinship, and the ideology of tribal
unity. Instead, the area is an atomistic, territorially defined region
with little genealogical depth and little traditional sociopolitical power
in the national arena. As we shall see, this was not a sociopolitical
environment conducive to the development of a new corporate entity
(i.e., an LDA) charged with the responsibility for managing the public affairs of local rural development.

RURAL DEVELOPMENT AND THE LOCAL
DEVELOPMENT ASSOCIATIONS

The main vehicle for promoting development in the rural areas of
Yemen are the LDAs, which were created early in the 1970s within
these contrasting local sociopolitical environments. Therefore, much
of the variance in development between the *qada*'s of Anis and Rayma
can be accounted for by examining the contrasting histories of the
two LDAs and how they functioned as corporate groups.

Anis Local Development Association

The Anis Local Development Association was established in 1970 by a small group of educated young men (the *shabab*), most of whom were employed in Sana'a. Faced with the fact that the postrevolutionary central government was very limited in its ability to provide much in the way of development assistance to the rural parts of the country, the cooperative movement began to concentrate on improving local conditions. Ideologically, the local development movement was derived from traditional concepts of cooperation (*'ayana*), probably reinforced by examples of cooperative movements in other parts of the developing world.[3] The first cooperatives were formed by the newly educated elites, who had a wider knowledge of international events than existed before the revolution. The initial idea for cooperative self-help associations, which had arisen in the 1960s in the form of local welfare associations, was developed by this younger generation, known commonly throughout Yemen as the "children of the revolution" (*wilad ith-thawra*). In the beginning of the Anis association, an administrative committee was formed to decide the kind of leadership that should be involved in the LDA, what qualifications the leaders should have, and what areas should be included in the association. Despite the fact that the LDA originated among the progressive youth who had a tendency toward rejection of the old political order associated with the tribal system, the committee decided that the association should be formed along the traditional tribal lines, instead of state administrative lines. This was done out of respect for the tribal traditions of Anis and out of recognition that Anis formed a political entity with historical depth and a strong sense of common identity.

According to the president of the Anis Local Development Association (in 1983), the administrative committee selected its initial leadership according to the following criteria.

The most prominent members of the local development board were to be important figures in the national political scene. By placing their most prominent leaders in the LDA, it was felt that the organization could get the most assistance from the state and obtain the necessary approval for projects in the most direct and quickest manner possible. The idea was to utilize the political connections of its most prominent members for public benefit. Traditional social status, such as shaykh, *sayyid*, or *qabili*, would not be an important consideration for LDA office.

The second criterion was that the leaders of the LDA be educated (*mutᶜallim*), with proven experience (*mutafanni*) in negotiations and with the ability to improvise plans quickly when and if opposition was encountered.

The last criterion was that the leaders of the LDA were to be from different regions within Anis so that the LDA would represent the tribe as a whole and not be dominated by just one section.

When the first LDA board was convened, it consisted primarily of young professionals. The initial Anis LDA included the following members: (1) a member of Parliament who later became minister of social affairs and labor and secretary general of the Confederation of Yemen Development Associations (CYDA); (2) the director of administration and finance, Ministry of Social Affairs and Labor; (3) the director of administration, finance, and drilling, Ministry of Agriculture; (4) the director of customs; (5) the director of employee affairs, Ministry of Agriculture; (6) a student at Sanaᶜa University; and (7) a captain (later colonel) in the Yemen Army (Green 1975). They were all from the ranks of the tribesmen (*qaba'il*); none of the traditional leaders, the *masha'ikh*, were elected to the first local development board. This caused some superficial tension between what could be described as the emerging class of young professionals (*shabab*) and the *masha'ikh*, who felt they were being left out. As a protest, the *masha'ikh* challenged the vote count, but it was proven to be accurate. The first board soon began working on the initial project, the Maᶜbar-Anis road.

One reason for the acceptance of the LDA by the traditional leaders was that all of the members were very successful men from important families (*al-ᶜayan*) with deep roots in the region. Although not *masha'ikh*, they were from families that had long played important roles in the organization and functioning of the tribe. Additionally, they were among the best-educated and brightest men in the tribe. Finally, the initial performance of the first local development board was of such a high caliber that its members were quickly accepted as leaders of the LDA.

The Anis LDA worked very well for over a decade, and many of its goals were attained. A permanent office was furnished and staffed in Sanaᶜa, and some technical assistance was obtained by hiring regional expatriates (e.g., from Sudan) to manage day-to-day operations such as bookkeeping. By maintaining LDA headquarters in Sanaᶜa, rather than in the countryside, the Anis LDA could effectively lobby the central government for technical and financial assistance as well as maintain very close ties to CYDA.

The initial focus of the Anis LDA was on developing a transportation network in the region, and the first project was the construction of the Maᶜbar–Suq al-Jumaᶜ–Madinat ish-Shirq road, begun in 1972 and finished in 1975. This road followed the traditional pathway that connected the major population centers in Anis. Later projects focused on construction of secondary roads, especially in the rugged mountainous regions in western Anis. Secondary priorities were in the fields of education and health; in 1978, the LDA-funded health clinic in Madinat ish-Shirq was completed.

LDA projects were organized according to five-year plans; by the time of the second LDA planning period, 1982–84, the initial road projects had been completed and most of Anis had been accessed by secondary roads. What remained to be done was construction of smaller roads to the more isolated areas, as well as needed improvements in the health and education areas.

In 1981, a central government policy shift by CYDA encouraged the breakup of the larger LDAs into smaller, district-level associations. This was done in order to encourage more balanced national competition among the LDAs for central government assistance and to lessen the power of the larger LDAs like Anis. The subject of splitting the Anis LDA into three separate associations (one for each *nahiya*—Dawran, Jabal ish-Shirq, and Maᶜbar/Jahran) was discussed, and the board agreed to comply with the CYDA directive. The breakup of the LDA into smaller units at this time was not the result of any serious internal problems within the Anis organization, but more out of practicality and conformance with CYDA policy.

For a long time, residents of Maᶜbar/Jahran had not been getting much direct benefit from the LDA. This part of Anis was a flat plains region, and its road construction was completed quickly. During the first decade, Maᶜbar/Jahran continued contributing to the Anis LDA, which was primarily occupied with building roads in the mountainous western regions, out of a sense of duty to the whole tribe of Anis. Once the western road projects were accomplished, it was agreed that each district could afford to finance its own projects

based on its own revenue-generating capacities and that more localized organization would be appropriate. Dawran and Jabal ish-Shirq
still had road construction and maintenance as their highest priorities, while Ma ͨbar/Jahran, having already built adequate roads, wanted
to shift toward developing the health and education infrastructure of
the subregion.

During the discussions over the breakup of Anis LDA, three
opinions emerged. One argued for the retention of the original Anis
LDA because its size and unity gave it strength in competition against
other LDAs and because it was a symbol of the tribe and reflected
the history of the unity of the area. The second opinion was that the
interests of the subregions within Anis were different due to the
physical nature of the areas and that it was more appropriate for
each to address the principal needs of the community more directly.
The third opinion was from the only shaykh on the local development board. He supported the breakup into three separate associations because he felt that this would create more offices and open
new opportunities to launch local political careers.

In the elections that followed restructuring, Dawran again elected
leaders based on personal criteria—professionals such as engineers,
university-educated young men, and military officers. In Ma ͨbar/
Jahran, and Jabal ish-Shirq, some of the *masha'ikh* were elected to
the LDA; thus, after a decade, some LDA power sharing was established between the young professionals (*shabab*) and the traditional
leaders (it happened that the *masha'ikh* elected also had personal
qualifications for the positions, and thus it was not purely a power
grab). An open competition based on a popular vote resulted in the
increase in membership among the *masha'ikh* in Ma ͨbar-Jahran
nahiya.

It is perhaps unusual that the Anis LDA, from its inception, was
run by the most qualified members of the *qada'*; by design, it was
also a tribally based association that used traditional tribal loyalties
as a means of inspiring cooperation. Although Anis was a very large
area, and all sections of the *qada'* were in need of development,
there was no serious infighting; nor were projects concentrated in
one specific area or group on political grounds. Instead, planning
was carried out with the intention of bringing as much benefit to the
whole region as possible. For example, the Ma ͨbar-Anis road opened
about two-thirds of the *qada'* to motorized transport. Also, the first

health center financed by the local development association was in
Madinat ish-Shirq, a market town in a very centralized location that
the planners felt would benefit the most people, including those
from other *qada's*. Since its beginnings, the Anis LDA has been one
of the most successful in all Yemen. The high rate of progress in
rural development in Anis is directly attributable to the efficient
functioning of the cooperative.

Jibal Rayma Local Development Association

The Jibal Rayma Local Development Association was formed in late
1972. Like the LDA in Anis, it was among the first group of cooperatives formed in the country. It also was organized according to
qada' and included five *nahiyas*—al-Jabin, Kusma, as-Salafiya, Bilad
it-Ta'am, and al-Ja'fariya. However, the Jibal Rayma LDA was different from the Anis LDA in many respects. First of all, the original
officers on the local development board were all traditional local leaders, that is, from the *masha'ikh*. The major force in the formation of
the LDA was a high-ranking military officer who was closely related
to the paramount shaykh of the *qada'*. During the first elections, the
only candidates were the *masha'ikh* of the five *nahiyas*, all allies of
the paramount shaykh. In contrast to Anis, guidelines for the qualifications of the LDA officers were not drawn up.

By 1975, after three years of operation, only a handful of projects
had been completed: five primary schools—one in each of the district centers. Plans had been drawn up for the construction of a roadway from the Tihama to al-Jabin, but work had not begun. Admin-
istratively, the Jibal Rayma LDA did not accomplish very much. It
did not establish permanent offices in Sana'a near the ministries and
CYDA; nor did it hire a professional staff. The cooperative remained
rural-based, without close ties to CYDA or the ministries.

Dissatisfaction was growing throughout the Jibal Rayma *qada'*
with the inefficiency of the LDA, and rumors were spreading that
the cooperative officials were "eating" (*akl*) the LDA funds. Additionally, it appeared that al-Jabin, the home district of the LDA
president, was drawing undue benefit from the cooperative. The main
road project, the construction of the Kuwaiti government-funded
school, and a British health project were all placed in al-Jabin
nahiya.

In 1977, a movement began among the younger intellectuals (*shabab*) in opposition to the Jibal Rayma LDA. Their main complaint was that the LDA was, in effect, entirely in the hands of one important shaykh and his followers. They felt that the Jibal Rayma LDA was not operating in accordance with the principles of the cooperative movement, that is, the "democratic participation of the people in electing general assemblies, boards of cooperative associations, coordination councils, and the confederation, as well as participation in drafting the plans, programs, and various affairs of the association" (YARG 1982:187). Instead, the Jibal Rayma LDA was felt by many to be the private enterprise of the paramount shaykh, who was using it for the benefit of his constituents.

In 1978, a group of five young men from Kusma *nahiya* decided to break away and establish an independent local development association. One of the reasons given for the breakup was that Kusma was the most agriculturally productive district and, in turn, produced the most tax revenues for the Jibal Rayma LDA, but was not getting a fair return. The five organizers included a successful merchant, a director of schools, and small business operators who were all known for their reason (*ᶜaql*). None of them were *masha'ikh*, and the head of the group was from a family who lived in the market. By February 1978, they had successfully petitioned CYDA in Sanaᶜa to form their own *nahiya* LDA, and general elections were held. Out of a maximum of sixty possible votes, the head organizer of the breakaway movement (a successful merchant from the Kusma market) gained all sixty, and the other four organizers were also elected by a large majority. In contrast, one of the more visible shaykhs who stood for election only managed to get five votes. Not one shaykh was elected.

This action broke the strength of the Jibal Rayma LDA, and it was then divided into five *nahiya* LDAs. Conflict between the traditional *masha'ikh* and the *shabab* erupted, which had a further retarding effect on the pace of local development projects. This process can be seen in a detailed description of the progress of the Kusma LDA.

In 1978, the first annual budget of the new Kusma LDA was reported to be 2 million rials. The LDA board decided that the money would be best spent on constructing a road through the *nahiya*. A road was the number one priority of the Kusma LDA because the area was mountainous and only accessible by long, arduous walks. Up to that time, all goods had to be brought into the region by donkey or hauled on the backs of porters, making the cost of manufactured items in the region higher than in other areas of Yemen.

The first serious problem encountered was trying to decide the route of the roadway. The LDA board wanted the most direct route to the summit and the district center at Kusma, which could be approached either from the east via Wadi Rima^c or by following the traditional footpath from Suq ^cAluja in the Tihama. However, these routes faced opposition. Almost all *^cuzla* representatives argued that the road should be through their particular subdistrict. Due to this competition, the planning process became bogged down for nearly a year.

Finally, a compromise was reached. Two roads were planned—one from the east, where the slope of the mountain was more gradual, and one from the west, up the steepest part of the mountain. Two bulldozers were purchased, along with some jackhammers, compressors, and the like. Also, an engineer was hired to do cost estimates. He evaluated three routes: one from the west, one from the east, and one from the south. The western route was estimated to cost 35 million rials; the eastern route, 5 million rials; and the southern route, about 15 million rials. The cost-effective route would have been from the east and would eventually have been connected to the Wadi Rima^c project (a central government venture), where an improved road (professionally graded and eventually paved) was planned. In spite of this, local pressure groups insisted that the western approach and the eastern approach be undertaken simultaneously. Work began in early 1979, but the first budget was soon exhausted. In all, only about ten kilometers of road were constructed; by 1983, not one single village had been accessed by the western road. In 1979, the second budget was approved, similar in size, but problems occurred that delayed all work.

In 1982, the road from al-Jabin approached the Kusma border, the eastern approach was abandoned, and a branch road from the al-Jabin road was started. By December 1983, this road was still two hours' walking distance from the district center, while the initial ^cAluja-Kusma road from the west had only reached the unpopulated lower slopes. If the initial eastern approach road had been constructed, the residents on the upper slopes of the mountain would have been connected to the road network years earlier; but nearly six years after the plans were made, they were still without a road. By insisting on being the first served, in effect, those on the western slopes of the mountain had become the last to benefit from the road construction project. The overall development in their part of the region had been severely hindered.

The case of the Kusma road is characterized by the lack of an overarching cooperative spirit. This failure is a direct result of the fragmented, atavistic sociopolitical environment in Jibal Rayma. Public interest and rational planning were sacrificed to appease the self-interested demands of local groups. The result was three partially completed roads, two of which are still useless.

Apart from the problem of planning and implementing the roads due to discord caused by the self-interest of each of the *ᶜuzla*s, the Kusma LDA also suffered from intense conflict between local political factions that caused a complete work stoppage between 1979 and 1981. The problem began in 1978 when a shaykh from an *ᶜuzla* northeast of Kusma, whom we shall call shaykh ᶜAli, got into a confrontation with some of the *shabab* in the *nahiya*. Shaykh ᶜAli, who was a close ally of the paramount shaykh in Jibal Rayma, was still stinging from his resounding defeat in the Kusma elections. According to informants, in order to bolster his self-esteem, he began to form his own small armed force. By manipulating his friendship with the *mudir an-nahiya*, as well as through alleged bribery, he got the personal use of a couple of soldiers who were assigned to the government post (*hukuma*) in Kusma center. The news of this private police force quickly spread around the *nahiya*. Two young men, one from Shaᶜaf (near Kusma) and one from an *ᶜuzla* in eastern Kusma *nahiya*, who were more progressive in their political beliefs went to Shaykh ᶜAli and confronted him. They argued that the two soldiers belonged in the district center, that the soldiers were public servants for all the people, and that he had no right to retain them as his personal security force (it was customary to pay a stipend to government soldiers in the event they were needed to arrest someone or settle a conflict, but he was getting their services free of charge). The two young men demanded the soldiers be returned to the *hukuma*. Shaykh ᶜAli refused, a fight broke out, and he was beaten up. The soldiers did not enter into the fracas.

It was known that the two young men were friends of the newly elected LDA leaders, although they themselves were not local leaders. Shaykh ʿAli assumed that they were acting as agents of the LDA. This assertion was strongly denied by the LDA, which insisted that the young men acted on their own accord.

Shaykh ʿAli sent word of the problem to the paramount shaykh in al-Jabin, who was also the former Jibal Rayma LDA president and director of security for the *qada'*.[4] At the same time, he mustered all the support he could from his allies among the *masha'ikh* and the residents of his immediate *ʿuzla*.

Word of this quickly reached the Kusma LDA, which mobilized a support group. Kusma center is located in a saddle between two mountain peaks, Jabal Kusma and Jabal Barad, and each group took up a fortified position on the mountaintops. A state of war existed for about a month, until a contingent of soldiers sent by the director of security (at the request of the paramount shaykh in al-Jabin) arrived to settle the matter and thus ended the armed confrontation. The problem then began to take on a legal/political character.

Because the Kusma LDA was new and appeared to have serious problems, the matter was referred to the central headquarters of CYDA in Sanaʿa. To bolster its case, the LDA brought almost all of the *mughram* secretaries—about twenty—to complain about the actions of Shaykh ʿAli and his group. The secretaries testified that the LDA leaders had not instigated the problem, but rather were attacked by Shaykh ʿAli and his followers. Sensing that he was losing the case, Shaykh ʿAli began spreading leaflets outside of CYDA, causing some embarrassment to the headquarters. He was jailed for two months for illegal political campaigning, but his leaflets worked, and CYDA ordered that new elections be held in Kusma. Part of the decision was that the incumbent LDA officers could not stand for reelection.

Shaykh ʿAli was released, and it appeared that he had won a victory because he was still able to run for election. With strong backing from the paramount shaykh in al-Jabin, the new slate of officers elected to the LDA were once again all from the *masha'ikh* class, and Shaykh ʿAli became president. But he was not content with his victory and decided to pursue his campaign against the former LDA officers and the *mughram* secretaries who had testified against him in Sanaʿa.

Shaykh ʿAli's position of power and his connections to the *mudir* of the *nahiya* and director of finances enabled him to order that all

of the *mughram* secretaries resign their positions and that new secretaries be selected. However, if the secretaries would sign a statement that they renounced their allegiance to the first Kusma LDA,
they would be allowed to retain their positions. Most of the secretaries declined, and new "puppet" secretaries were placed in their positions. This was a clever move by Shaykh ᶜAli, because he knew that
there must be an audit of the yearly accounts whenever a new LDA
takes office; each line item in the accounts must be approved and
verified by the *mughram* secretaries, who are in charge of local tax
collection. Thus, when the time for the audit came, he had already
replaced all of the secretaries with his supporters. Although these
new secretaries knew nothing about the first LDA accounts or expenditures, at the instruction of Shaykh ᶜAli they challenged every line
item and declared the accounts out of balance. Shaykh ᶜAli engi-
neered a block vote against the original Kusma LDA, and it was
rumored that there was good evidence that these new secretaries were
bribed for their vote. The matter was taken to the CYDA court
(*niyaba*) in Sanaᶜa for hearing; the case was heard by two employees
of CYDA, who, according to one of the litigants, did not know the
proper procedures and mishandled the matters, perhaps also being
bribed by the *masha'ikh*. The period of litigation lasted from 1979
through 1980 (during which the LDA was suspended), and the decision rendered required the former LDA officials to make restitution
of around 60,000 rials apiece. They were also forbidden to run for
LDA offices in the future. Shaykh ᶜAli had won another round.

In January 1981, the governor of Sanaᶜa province, who is also the
president of the governorate LDA coordinating council (*majlis
it-tansiq*), was sent on a fact-finding mission to Kusma to investigate
the growing political problems with the National Democratic Front
and to discuss the problems with local leadership facing the district.
The case of the 60,000 rial judgment was brought to the governor's
attention by the former treasurer of the first Kusma LDA, who presented him with copies of all of the records of the LDA transactions
that took place during his time in office. The governor reviewed the
accounts, declared that they in fact had been in order, and there had
been no financial malfeasance on the part of the first Kusma LDA,
and canceled all of the debts imposed on the first LDA leaders by
the CYDA court. He then ordered that the LDA headed by Shaykh
ᶜAli be dissolved and that new elections be held. Also, for this elec-

tion, members of neither the first nor the second Kusma LDA were to be allowed to stand for office.

However, because of the past history of problems associated with the LDA, no one actually wanted to run for office for the third LDA. By this time, there was a also new *mudir* of the *nahiya*; after meeting with members of both former LDAs, it was agreed that a new slate of LDA candidates would be drafted and that it was to be composed of both *masha'ikh* and *shabab*. In the opinion of some of the Kusma residents, this new group was not very talented, but it was believed that it could get along in a mediocre fashion and could resume the long-stalled LDA projects—especially the roads.

The stormy history of the Kusma LDA clearly indicates the conflict between the traditional power elite and the younger, more educated, and progressive elements in Jibal Rayma. Factionalism was rife in Jibal Rayma, and there was little sense of unity or cohesiveness for public benefit. In the case of the Jibal Rayma LDAs, the traditional but recently disenfranchised *masha'ikh* clearly perceived the LDA as an important institution that had to be controlled in order to ensure their power, which, as we saw in chapter 5, had been steadily eroded since the revolution. Part of their perception that the LDA was usurping their power was based on the fact that residents of the area were taking their problems to the LDA leaders instead of to the *masha'ikh*—as had been customary in the prerevolutionary and civil war period—and they were steadily losing their clients. The following case illustrates this point.

ʿAbdul Karim was elected to the first Kusma LDA by a unanimous decision. Born in the town of Kusma, he was a shopkeeper who was not from a notable family, and there was a question about whether or not he was even of *qabili* status. He made a fortune in commodity trading with his brother and began building the largest, most modern house in Kusma. Additionally, he was head of the local chapter of the Muslim Brotherhood; he was known as a harsh, cold individual, but one of exceptional ability, business sense, and moral uprightness. After his election to the LDA, the tribesmen began to take their petitions to him for adjudication on matters involving customary law (ʿuruf), and he held daily court in the lower floor of his new home. As was the custom for any local leader, he began to receive money for his services as mediator, and his reputation for fairness caused his practice to increase. Consequently, the paralegal business of the *masha'ikh* began to decline, and they were not earning as much money in their traditional role as mediators.

This emergence of new political leadership associated with the office of the LDA was perceived by the *masha'ikh* as a threat and an erosion of traditionally held power and a means of making money. The matter was exacerbated because local leadership was switching from the traditional elites to individuals of exceptional ability, some of whom were even of questionable *qabili* ancestry.

In sum, in Jibal Rayma, there is colorful history of competition and conflict over the LDA leadership. Part of the problem stems from the fact that the traditional leaders, by assuming control of the LDA in its beginning phase, politicized the association. Their roles as leaders and adjudicators of disputes, which carried status and economic rewards, were mixed with their role as administrators of the public development funds. When the *shabab* LDA leaders came into office, the former elites once again began to lose some of their political power as leaders. The revolution was being played out again, this time on the local level. When the people began to take their problems to the new LDA leaders, the *masha'ikh* also began to lose a valued source of income, which prompted remedial action. This contributed to a level of disruption that severely retarded the progress of development in Jibal Rayma.

Second, there was no incipient corporate structure on which to base the Jibal Rayma LDAs. Cooperation had to be wrangled from a mass of small, atomistic groups that held their particular interests to be primary, making collective decision making and collective action quite difficult.

In the discussion of the political environment in Anis, by contrast, we saw that the LDA was only a nominal threat to the power base of the traditional elites. In fact, in Anis there had not been any significant shifts in power—the LDA was a new addition to the political scene that did not cut into the existing power structures. Additionally, Anis had a long history of occasional corporate action and the incipient corporate tribal structure on which to base the cooperative. The next chapter continues the discussion of local politics, exploring more fully the role of ideological factors in local development.

7

Ideology and Local Development

In addressing the differences in functioning of the LDAs in Anis and Jibal Rayma, additional insight may be gained by phrasing the question in another manner. We might also ask: why didn't the emergence of the LDA touch off significant competiton between the new class of politically aware educated professionals (the *shabab*) and the former elites in Anis to the degree that it did in Jibal Rayma? As argued in the last chapter, part of the answer is found on the materialist level, in the differences in the relations of power in the two districts. However, this is only one aspect of the picture. Significant contrasts can be drawn on the ideological level as well—differences in local ideologies that govern how local development activities are motivated and rationalized.

This chapter explores the argument that in Anis the tribe was a successful base on which to organize the LDA because it provided an ideology of unity and cooperation that could be adapted as a basis for wide-scale collective action. The tribe of Anis has a long history of occasional group action in matters of common defense, economic help, traditional public works projects, and mutual support in times of crisis. Additionally, certain key tribal values encapsulated in the tribal ideology (*qabayla*), especially the concept of *ʿayana*, reinforced the ideals of community cooperation and self-help that were the ideological cornerstones of the LDA movement. Most importantly, the tribe—as the highest expression of putative kinship—served, through the genealogical idiom, to unite the residents of various ecological zones (mountains, plains, and wadis) into one unit.

Rural Yemen has a social environment naturally prone to competitiveness. As very telling evidence of this underlying potential for divisiveness and factionalism, one need only examine the architecture of the highlands—carefully designed for defensive purposes (Serjeant and Lewcock 1983:464). The development needs for each ecological zone, and often each community, vary according to availability of important resources (e.g., water supplies, arable land). The institution of the tribe, through putative and real kinship links, serves a tension-management function that allows for an expanded perspective of who can be considered group members. The positive influence of a shared tribal identity on local development in Anis can be seen in the way it provided a rationale that could be actively manipulated to justify the concentration of LDA resources in the areas with the greatest need (i.e., the western mountain regions of Anis). It was possible to convince the residents of Anis to approve funneling development resources into the more remote regions by positing the argument that the entire tribe was strengthened by the improvement of services in the peripheral areas.

In describing the levels of cooperation and solidarity in Anis, it would, however, be misleading to assume that the area was not subject to the kinds of internecine tensions and feuding that affected most other regions in Yemen. Indeed, this is not the case. Certainly, disputes were endemic to the region, as some of the examples in chapter 5 indicate, and occasionally they had negative consequences for local development. For example, some rural roads were left unconnected to others because of localized conflicts between tribal segments. One informant described the tension between residents of Bani Khalid and al-ᶜAir in western Anis due to a long-standing disagreement over territorial boundaries and water rights.

The LDA planning committee had proposed a roadway that would connect Bani Khalid (Dawran district) with al-ᶜAir and Maghrabit al-ᶜAnis (Jabal ish-Shirq district) by the shortest and most direct route. This would transect portions of each subdistrict. The residents of al-ᶜAir refused to allow the roadway through their territory because the area was often used by their women for collecting firewood and they feared that the women would be subject to possible harassment in the event that the conflict between the regions again escalated. As a result, a much longer and more expensive route was chosen and resources that could have been put to better use were tied up in a more costly and time-consuming project.

In other instances, feeder roads were not connected in order to protect regional markets. For example, the residents of the community Hadran overlook Wadi Rima^c and the main suq of Madinat ish-Shirq. A road was constructed to the bottom of a branch of the wadi, but the last 100 meters that would have connected it to the main road were not completed. The merchants of Suq al-Juma^c at the summit of Jabal ish-Shirq were afraid that they would lose most of the business from Hadran, so they blocked funding for the final link of the road. As a result, the roadway became a long dead-end, which, although useful for the residents of Hadran to reach Suq al-Juma^c, did not provide for the most direct route to the nearest major market.

Although problems and conflicts occurred in Anis, with occasionally serious negative consequences for local development, they were never so intense as to severely impede the overall local development movement in the entire subprovince. Additionally, the Anis LDA, in cooperation with the tribal leadership, was usually able to resolve the disputes in a manner agreeable to all parties.

In sum, the Anis cooperative consciously sought to utilize the positive aspects of the tribe, as a unifying traditional feature of the sociopolitical organization of the region, in order to reduce the potential for competition and factionalism indigenous to highland Yemen. To achieve this goal, the somewhat archaic administrative division of the *qada'*, which happened to correspond exactly to the tribe, was used to define the LDA, thereby giving the tribe a legitimate legal administrative basis for forming its LDA. Ensuring that all of the *nahiya*s within the *qada'* (and therefore all of the major subdivisions of the tribe) were represented on the local development board, stressing the historical unity of the tribe and its tradition of acting as one entity, and emphasizing the meaning of the tribe led to a generalized sentiment that all of the people formed one political unit. Thus, the Anis LDA successfully coalesced into a well-functioning modern cooperative. The institution of the tribe and its accompanying ideology was one feature among many others that contributed in a positive manner to the development of a successful association in Anis.

In contrast, Jibal Rayma did not have the unifying factor of the tribe on which to base its local development association. Lacking this traditional basis for formation of a modern corporate group, Jibal Rayma was left to build its LDA on an already-factionalized base.

The problems and conflicts over allocation of LDA resources, which were successfully smoothed over in Anis by invoking tribal sentiments, were not as easily resolved, since the genealogical idiom, the basic tribal mechanism for motivating group action and unity, was absent. The prevailing social conditions of factionalism and limited loyalties primarily restricted to the family and the village cluster were not mediated or tempered by higher-level traditional organizations such as the tribe. The numerous small communities, given at times to intense competition over limited resources, were involved in infighting over leadership and representation in the LDA, as well as over the allocation of the development projects. In the end, resolution of these disputes was only achieved by the arbitration of outside authorities.

TRADITIONAL IDEOLOGIES AND DEVELOPMENT

As often noted in the literature on rural development and cooperatives, their success depends on ideological factors such as a sense of altruism (Worsley 1971:2), a collectivist orientation, and a limitation of self-interest. Such attitudes and values, it has been shown, are part and parcel of society in both Anis and Jibal Rayma, albeit at different levels. *ʿAyana*, the basic idea of cooperation, is evident in customs like *ja'ish* and *faza*—examples of a traditional ethic of group participation and collective work for public benefit. As Adra (1982:121) has shown, these are basic tribal values and are part of the ethical system of *qabayla*, shared by all who consider themselves tribal (*qabili*). This holds true even in areas without the formal institution of the tribe. However, these values derive from the tribe itself and are predicated on the belief that the tribe is in essence like one large family, a point continually stressed by informants. In Yemen—and in the Middle East in general, as reflected in the often quoted bromide, "I against my brother; my brother and I against my cousins; my brother, my cousins, and I against the whole world"—loyalties and alliances exist in an ascending order, beginning with the immediate family and extending outward to include the larger units of social organization. Traditional ideas of cooperation are supported and reinforced by the tribal structure based on putative kinship and political history.

The people in Jibal Rayma, although "tribesmen" in terms of social status because most members trace their family heritage to some recognized tribe, were not closely or historically related to each other. Therefore, the traditional tribal sentiments and values that predicated cooperation on a generalized sense of kinship unity were not nearly as strong there. When the number and intensity of vertical ties are compared between the regions, Anis, with the institution of the tribe uniting the region, far surpasses Jibal Rayma. In view of the arguments of Barakat (1977), Widstrand (1972), and Worsley (1971) cited earlier, the cases of Anis and Jibal Rayma in the western central highlands of Yemen do not support their conclusions that traditional sociopolitical organizations based on vertical ties are de facto detrimental to the development of modern cooperatives.

In Anis, the vertical ties based on the genealogical model functioned in three ways. First, they reduced tensions inherent in the region due to ecological and demographic conditions. Second, these ties provide a rationale to legitimize the skewed distribution of development projects, thus reducing resentment and possible in-group competition. Third, and most importantly, they reinforced the idea that the LDA was also a reflection of the integrity and unity of the tribe itself. In contrast, the scattered mountain communities of Jibal Rayma were continually embroiled in local conflicts over the LDA and its projects, and this proved to be detrimental to the functioning of the cooperative.

LEADERSHIP, STATUS, AND DEVELOPMENT

Another important dimension of traditional sociopolitical organizations included in the analysis of Barakat (1977) and Widstrand (1972) is the issue of leadership. According to their arguments, leadership in traditional social organization is based upon ascribed status rather than on achievement; consequently, circulation of leaders is restricted. Those most qualified are often excluded from participation on the basis of social status. Seibel and Massing's (1974) research on the cooperative movement in Liberia also focuses attention on the importance of achieved versus ascribed status in the rural development process. In their study, a higher rate of success was noted in regions of Liberia where traditional leadership in the segmentary lineage system was based on personal achievement than in the regions where leadership was based on ascribed status. Implied in their argument is the notion that the traditional sociopolitical environment has an important determining influence on the emergence of successful local cooperatives.

This issue is of importance for Yemen because the hierarchical traditional system of social stratification is predicated on a folk model that defines and limits one's position in the social system according to descent (i.e., ascribed status). An important question, therefore, is whether or not the social system restricts the emergence of new leadership and what effects, if any, this may have had on rural development, particularly the local development associations.

Although the basic categories in the social hierarchy are ascribed, there is evidence to indicate that leadership roles have traditionally been accorded on the basis of personal achievement. We may take, for example, the office of the shaykh. On the surface, the system of tribal leadership (*masha'ikh*) has the appearance of being based purely upon ascription; the office of shaykh frequently passes down within the same family. However, new political careers often emerge within the traditional system. Through a process of consensus, new shaykhs are "elected" to represent the tribe, tribal group, or tribal area in public matters (see chapter 5). There is no ideological base for the status of shaykh according to ascribed criteria as there is, for example, with major social status categories such as *sayyid*, *qabili*, or *akhdam*. Although it may come to appear to be an ascribed status, the higher status accorded a shaykh is first and foremost the result of his having achieved a local reputation and title. The shaykh has, in essence, only the ascribed status of *qabili* (tribesman).

The evidence from Anis and Jibal Rayma, as well as other regions of Yemen, indicates that the tribal system is more open to a circulation of leadership than the traditional systems characterized by Barakat (1977) and Widstrand (1972). When the Anis LDA was formed along tribal lines, and it was decided that there would be open competition for offices, this did not constitute a radical social innovation — nor did it run counter to basic tribal values. Discussions with informants from Anis indicate that leadership based on personal achievement has consistently been a legitimate part of the tribal system, as seen by both the tribesmen and the *masha'ikh*, and was tolerated in Anis so long as the *masha'ikh* were not categorically excluded from LDA office.[1] As a result, the LDA leadership in Anis was composed of people with technical and administrative skills drawn mostly from the ranks of the tribesmen (*qaba'il*), but also eventually came to include a few officers from the *masha'ikh* who were elected on the basis of their individual expertise rather than their social status.

In Jibal Rayma, where the first LDA was made up entirely of *masha'ikh*, I initially had the impression that there were reasons rooted in the traditional ideology that accounted for this situation. However, upon examination of the allocation of positions of influence in the postrevolutionary local administration, this proved not to be the case. For example, in Kusma *nahiya* average tribesmen held the positions of head of municipalities, director of finance, director of schools, director of the clinic, and most of the ᶜ*uzla* or *mughram* secretaries. These men were assigned or elected to the positions on the basis of their personal qualifications. Local leadership was not confined to the *masha'ikh* in the postrevolutionary period of state building in Yemen. The initial Jibal Rayma LDA was composed of *masha'ikh* because it was organized by a prominent shaykh with high military ranking who enlisted the support of his client group, the various *masha'ikh* of the region. In the formative stages of the Jibal Rayma LDA, little attention was paid to setting out specific criteria for membership, and there was no widespread interest among the residents of Jibal Rayma in the internal structure of the association. As a result, there were no candidates for office other than the paramount shaykh and his clients. Once the association began work and gained official access to public funds, interest spread within the region; other educated residents began to focus a critical eye on the functioning of the association. They began comparing the progress of the Jibal Rayma LDA with other regions and realized that there were serious problems. When they started to exert pressure to secure correction and improvement within the association, their opposition was viewed more in political than in administrative terms and quickly polarized the *masha'ikh* and the young, educated residents (*shabab*).

When the subsequent elections were held after the breakup of the Jibal Rayma LDA into five *nahiya* associations, any individual was allowed to stand for election, and candidates then came to include ordinary tribesmen and merchants, as well as members of the *masha'ikh*. The defeat of the tight in-group of *masha'ikh* was due to dissatisfaction with their initial performance and growing political awareness that the *masha'ikh* in Jibal Rayma were trying to regain the local power they had lost through the 1962 revolution by controlling the LDA and its tax base. The *shabab* gained the support of the people because they showed considerable organizational and administrative talent by successfully engineering the breakup of the Jibal Rayma LDA into the five *nahiya* associations.

A recurrent theme in the more theoretical literature on development is the potentially disruptive effect traditional elites may have on the development process (Nash 1959:137–50; Cohen 1968:75; Foster 1973:1). Elites like the *masha'ikh* in Yemen are often viewed as conservative elements in the traditional social system that block the attempts at social change by more progressive elements or thwart development efforts by using their political power to control development funds or projects to enhance their own local careers or benefit local clients. In the case of Jibal Rayma, this was perceived by the locals as a particular problem, but not in the case of Anis. Greed, self-interest, and the desire to protect vested interests are often assumed to be motivations for traditional elites to control development projects. Although on an individual level there is variability, the real crux of the matter lies in the very nature of the social role and power of traditional elites.

From the beginning of the LDA in Anis, the traditional elites were on the periphery of the movement and not directly threatened by the LDA usurping their traditional leadership functions. The concerns of the LDA were new and outside the usual domain of the traditional leaders. An anecdote may illustrate this point.

My initial contact with the community of Dawran Anis regarding the possibilities of developing a primary health care project in the region was made by arranging an appointment with the shaykh of the region. After I explained the intentions of the project, he asked why I came to him, and suggested that I should have spoken with the LDA itself. The implication was clear that he had little to do with such concerns. The situation of the LDA in Anis was similar to that reported by Colletta (1979) with the Sarvodaya associations in Sri Lanka, where a dual system emerged, one segment consisting of traditional elites maintaining their traditional functions and a second segment concerned with the new development activities. This separation of the LDA leadership from the *masha'ikh* in Anis allowed for the emergence of the cooperative without the negative effects of internal competition that are endemic in the traditional tribal leadership system. In Jibal Rayma, the problem was not avoided because the initial LDA leadership consisted entirely of the *masha'ikh*. True to form, each shaykh tried to direct LDA resources into his own region, with the resulting unequal distribution of resources and poor planning.

Writers on Yemeni social organization have also commented that among tribesmen there is an egalitarian ideology that all *qabili* are essentially equal in status, although there are other criteria (e.g., prestige, wealth, reputation, *hajj*, etc.) that are important in determining patterns of interaction (Gerholm 1977:110; Stevenson 1981:141; Adra 1982:81; Tutwiler 1987). Even in regard to the shaykh, Adra reports that the tribesmen "talk to their own *shaykh*s as equals with their heads held high" (1982:81) and that the tribesmen ideally regard the shaykh as "first among equals." This ideal of equality (*musawa'a*) was expressed to me by an educated resident of Anis in discussions about the possibility of dominance of the Anis LDA by the *masha'ikh*:

> Most of the Anis people are from big and important families and, regardless of occupation, took pride in the family and tribal heritage, and I do not think that the dominance of any family could have had any significant influence in the election of a member to the LDA. The important thing was the elected person himself. Was he an educated person with ability and experience to serve his area and did he have a good reputation, strong and influential personality, a good record and altruistic attitude?

Despite differences in individual successes, as long as one was a member of the tribe and the family heritage was noble, all tribesmen were theoretically equal. The explanation that the egalitarian ideal among tribesmen (*qaba'il*) functioned to support open circulation of leaders in the local development associations is reasonable, so long as we remember that they were drawn from the ranks of the tribesmen to whom the ideal directly applied. But the issue is made more complex by the fact that members of the merchant class (*baya^c in*, *tujjar*), generally regarded as lower in social rank, also participated in the LDA. To what extent can this be attributed to the tribal egalitarian ideology?

This question requires consideration of how traditional tribal values continue to operate in a changing cultural environment. One important fact to keep in mind is that—with the changes brought about since the revolution, particularly high emigration, increased public education, and the change from a basically subsistence to a cash-oriented economy — many of the traditional barriers between social status groups have been gradually disintegrating. Although some of the more symbolic aspects of status distinctions, such as the reluctance to intermarry, appear to remain strong, the closer associations between tribesmen and the nontribal people of the market have resulted in some important changes in attitudes about the importance of ascribed social status. A significant reason for this has been the entrance of the tribesmen into the commercial arena of shopkeeping and trade, occupations traditionally considered beneath their dignity. In a very real sense, the tribesmen have had to learn rational management and business practices from the merchant class in order to be competitive in the market. The result has been closer interpersonal ties and, to some extent, the emergence of different patterns of socializing. It is now common practice for merchants in the rural suqs to spend the afternoon chewing qat while minding the store, and neighboring shopkeepers, often from different social backgrounds, spend these hours in each other's company.

Based on descriptions by western central highlanders, the expatriate work environment in which the emigrant lives was something of a melting pot. While abroad, Yemenis from the same area but different social backgrounds live and work together; thus, closer relations have developed. In postrevolutionary Yemen, the increase in rural education also seems to have contributed to changing attitudes. The first rural schools were constructed in the larger settlements, district centers, and markets where, coincidentally, most nontribal people maintained their livelihood. Because, as guaranteed in the Yemeni constitution, education was open to all (YARG 1971:article 32), students of both tribal and nontribal background were brought together and placed in competitive school environments where success is based on achievement rather than on social status. The result of these postrevolutionary changes has been the partial fusion of these social status groups, particularly in professional and economic life.

In many regions of Yemen, including Anis, the initial organizers of the cooperatives were among the more progressive "children of the revolution" (*wilad ith-thawra*) who took very seriously the principles of equality outlined in the Yemeni constitution (YARG 1971:articles 8, 19, 36). I was on many occasions criticized by these tribesmen for using such well-known terms as *naqqis*, *bani khums*, and *akhdam* that refer to ranking in the traditional social hierarchy, because they reflect the old order and were felt to cast present-day Yemen in a bad light. The point was often made that all are citizens of Yemen and all are equal. Although one cannot say that the viewpoint of the *wilad ith-thawra* represents the mainstream of thought on the matter of social stratification, it is representative of the opinion of the majority who were involved in the Anis and breakaway Kusma cooperatives. Tutwiler (1984) in his study of the LDA in Mahwit province (an area north of this research area) reports a similar ideology, which he refers to as "revolutionary tribalism," in which the traditional emphasis on social rank, birth, and kinship are downplayed, while the notion of being tribal (*qabili*) is retained and emphasized. This change in ideology is certainly a growing trend.

Whether or not the egalitarian tribal ideal was part of the value system that supported the policy decision to include the members of the merchant stratum in the LDA leadership of Anis and the reformed LDAs of Jibal Rayma or whether the social changes outlined above were primarily responsible is difficult to ascertain. Most likely both were important, but the evidence from examination of the composition of the elected leaders of the LDAs in this study indicates that status differences based on ascribed criteria, often considered as a part of the Yemeni "tribal" social system, did *not* play that significant a role in restricting the emergence of new leadership in the LDAs. Actually, the evidence indicates that, in the changing context of Yemeni society, the tribal egalitarian ideal was quite consistent with the policy of open leadership adopted by the LDAs and was expanded to include other members of society.

SECTARIAN POLITICS AND DEVELOPMENT

A second ideological factor in Yemen that has relevance for the discussion of local development is religious sectarianism. In Yemen, the three main religious sects are the Zaydi and Isma ͨili (sometimes called Mukarrami) sects of the Shi ͨa branch of Islam and the Shafi ͨi school of Sunni Islam. The Zaydis are primarily concentrated in the northern and central highlands and the eastern desert regions of Yemen. A rough demarcation line between the Zaydi and Shafi ͨi regions runs east to west from just below Sumara Pass and north to south between the westernmost mountain ranges. The coastal plains and the southern regions near the border of the People's Democratic

Republic of Yemen are also predominantly Shafiᶜi. The Ismaᶜili sect is limited to a small enclave in the mountainous Haraz region, Bani Ismaᶜil, and some of Hyma, all located about halfway between Sanaᶜa and the port city of al-Hudayda.

Although there are many distinctions based on interpretation of religious law and custom, the differences between the two main branches of Islam, as expressed in Yemen society, are centered on the succession of the caliphate and the role of the imam in public affairs. The Shiᶜa argue that the proper line of succession to the caliphate was through ᶜAli, the nephew and son-in-law of the Prophet (as opposed to Muᶜawiya as the Sunni claim), and that the legitimate succession of the caliphate was limited only to the direct descendants of the Prophet (*ahl ab-Bayt*). There are some other differences in ritual observance, but these are considered of little importance in Yemen. From a purely ideological perspective, the Zaydi branch of Shiᶜa Islam, founded by Zayd ibn ᶜAli Abadin, the grandson of ᶜAli, the fourth caliph (successor) after the Prophet Muhammad, is so close to orthodox Sunni Islam that it is frequently referred to as the fifth school (*al-madhhab al-khamis*) of Islamic law (Wenner 1967:36). The Shafiᶜis, who are roughly equal in number with the Zaydis, reject the claim that the imam has authority on matters concerning dogma and only accept him as a temporal leader. Religious authority is not considered by the Shafiᶜis to be something inherited, but instead stems from religious acts (*sunna*) and from the religious community (*ᶜumma*).

The sectarian roots of political conflicts in Yemen run deep. In much of the Middle East, sectarian strife has been a common feature of social existence since medieval times. A cursory glance at the historical competition between the early Islamic states in Yemen reveals that political alliances between the tribes and the state were forged along sectarian lines. Solidarity based on a common religious belief was a means of uniting disparate tribal groups for the expansion of the Islamic state. With the ascendance of the Zaydi Imamate over the other early Islamic states, the seeds of sectarian discord were sown in the very structure of the state. From its beginnings under Imam al-Hadi in A.D. 882 until the 1962 revolution, the major state offices were under the control of the Zaydi *sayyid*s. Although at least half of Yemen was Shafiᶜi, the Zaydi-dominated administration controlled all of the avenues of political power. Taxation, imposed on all parts of Yemen, was under the direct control of the Zaydi imam, and there was little local delegation of power. Taxes were siphoned from the rural sector in support of the state machinery, and little was ever returned to the community to facilitate development or improvements. Yemen was politically dominated by the Zaydis for centuries, a situation that was often perceived as sectarian oppression.[2] In postrevolutionary Yemen, although it has been downplayed, sectarianism is still felt by some to be a basis of social injustice.[3]

Most recently, the perception of asymmetry of power, along with the underlying image of Zaydi domination, was an important factor in the rise of the National Democratic Front (*al-jubha al-wataniya ad-dimukratiya*) in 1980–81. The front was most active in the Shafi‘i regions of Dhamar and in ab-Bayda governorate, where it was able to gain considerable popular support by casting the conflict in sectarian terms in an attempt to rekindle resentments long entrenched during the time of the imam.[4]

Given the thousand-year history of the Zaydi/Shafi‘i split, it is reasonable to assume that these sectarian divisions have not ceased to be important in the modern state.[5] The issue of sectarianism and development has been given most attention by students of the Middle East who have analyzed the Lebanese situation. While I do not intend to develop a comparative analysis between Yemen and Lebanon per se, the relationship between sect and development should be examined in light of the literature on the Middle East.

Local development is an extremely complex phenomenon subject to a vast array of potential influences; in Yemen, sect and tribe have been of significance at different levels of sociopolitical organization, particularly the regional (governorate) and the local (district) levels. In order to understand how tribe and sect affected development in Yemen, it is important to keep in mind how development projects are financed and supported. Most, especially those implemented through the LDAs, are financed through a combination of locally generated revenues (*zakat* tax and direct contributions) and central government assistance or other outside contributions. If either the local or central government source is obstructed, long delays in the completion of the project invariably ensue. Local development involves interaction with associations and agencies from the most local committees (i.e., the individual LDA and villagers), to the regional bureaucracies (i.e., governorate coordinating council, *majlis it-tansiq*), and the relevant national agencies (i.e., CYDA and relevant ministries). Therefore, the potential for political manipulation of the development process exists at a number of levels.

Sectarian Politics

The Local Level

At the most local levels of social organization—that is, within the district or the tribe—sectarian differences rarely are of importance in daily affairs. When local administrative boundaries were drawn up under previous forms of administration (e.g., the Ottoman Turkish and imamic), attention was paid to maintaining traditional boundaries. As a result, there is sectarian homogeneity within most local units. In the fourteen western central highland districts in which I was able to conduct some research, only one district, ʿUtama, had a significant mix of both Zaydi and Shafiʿi residents. All of the others were either entirely Zaydi or Shafiʿi. Consequently, conflicts and disputes over leadership, distribution of development projects, and other problems within the district LDA were not related to sectarian issues. This situation is quite different from Lebanon, where the mixture of sects creates majority/minority tensions within each locality (Hudson 1968:26–27). In rural Yemen, sect really becomes an issue only at the higher levels of political organization.

The Regional Level

The situation is significantly different at the regional or governorate level, especially in those governorates that contain both Zaydi and Shafiʿi districts. Historically, Zaydi/Shafiʿi tensions were a main feature of Yemeni political life during the imamic period because important positions in the imam's administrative organization were filled by the Zaydi elites, who were reputed to have forced economic hardships on the Shafiʿi regions. Additionally, the Zaydi tribes, concentrated in the agriculturally less productive northern and eastern regions of Yemen, periodically launched raids against the more productive southern Shafiʿi regions (Halliday 1974). These tensions, historically important for the past thousand years, have continued into postrevolutionary Yemen and have been used by dissident groups, including the National Democratic Front (*al-jubha al-wataniya ad-dimukratiya*), to mobilize support for their causes. The 1980–82 confrontation between the government and the front was concentrated in the governorates of Sanaᶜa, Dhamar, and ab-Bayda, which have both Zaydi and Shafiᶜi districts.

The contrasting situations in *qada*'s Jibal Rayma and Anis afford the possibility of examining the potential for sectarian politics to affect rural development. Jibal Rayma, a completely Shafiᶜi *qada*', is located in Sanaᶜa governorate, where the majority of districts are Zaydi. On the other hand, Anis is a Zaydi *qada*' in Dhamar governorate, where the majority of districts are Zaydi. When sectarian composition is considered, Jibal Rayma is in the position of being in the minority within the governorate, while Anis forms part of the majority.

As mentioned, local development in Yemen is dependent on input from a number of sources; although the greatest portion of resources are generated locally, critical input can come from the central government and governorate-level agencies. Resources for development are funneled through national-level agencies (e.g., CYDA) to the governorate-level organizations (e.g., the coordinating council, *majlis it-tansiq*), and from there to the local level. This hierarchical system thus allows for significant control of the allocation of development resources at the governorate level, where the competition is often most intense.

In governorates such as Sanaᶜa and Dhamar, the existence of sectarian political blocks correlates with asymmetrical distribution of the centrally administered resources. This unevenness of distribution is often viewed as a consequence of sectarian favoritism and discrimination. The extent to which this is actually the case is difficult to prove, but in the minority regions, like Jibal Rayma, where development has seriously lagged behind, sectarian politics has been the main reason cited by the residents to account for the situation.

The people of Anis, in contrast, were among the Zaydi majority in their governorate, and informants there were of the opinion that sectarian differences were no longer really important in Yemeni social life and were particularly of little significance in the operation of the LDA governorate coordination council. One informant, who has high standing in the community and close associations with the local development association, went so far to demonstrate his point as to say that in prayer ritual the people in the region freely switched between Zaydi and Shafiᶜi styles—that they no longer consider themselves either Zaydi or Shafiᶜi, but simply Muslim. Sectarian discrimination, he felt, was a feature of prerevolutionary Yemen and no longer at issue.[6]

The people of Anis, as members of the Zaydi majority of their governorate, did not experience any sectarian disadvantages and consequently were able to take a more idealistic position. However, some evidence indicates that they were sensitive to the issue. They were cautious not to disclose publicly how many of the resources for development came from the central government for fear that the actual asymmetrical distribution of power and resources to the area would become known. A principal informant from Anis, who provided me with detailed accounts of LDA projects over the past few years, reported that cash amounts of central government contributions would not be provided by the LDA because the members "were afraid that it would become known how large they were and that in the future they would not be allocated such large sums." In Dhamar governorate, the most developed regions are the Zaydi areas, a correlation that is consistent with the assertions by members of the Shafiᶜi districts in the governorate that they receive a smaller share of the state revenues.

In Shafiᶜi Jibal Rayma, the attitude toward sectarian politics was quite different. Informants were unanimous in their opinion that the small amount of support for their development projects, the long delays they experienced in getting technical aid from CYDA through the governorate coordinating council, and problems in funding for their projects were due to sectarian politics. They claimed that the Zaydi governorate leaders were lining their pockets and channeling most of the resources to their own regions.

To what extent these allegations are based on the current political situation or are a holdover from times when sectarian politics were more visible is difficult to ascertain. But, along with informants' statements, examination of the distribution of health projects and schools in Sanaᶜa governorate yields some corroborating evidence. According to the Yemen government statistical yearbook, in 1979–80, within the six qada's that make up Sanaᶜa governorate there were 74 primary schools; but of these, only 5 were in qada' Jibal Rayma. When considering the distribution of schools according to population, Jibal Rayma, with 14 percent of the total for the governorate, had only 7 percent of the schools. Also, of the 350 medical doctors in the governorate in 1982, only 3 were in Jibal Rayma (one of whom was engaged in training and had no clinical practice); of the 86 rural health units in the governorate (YARG 1983*b*:256) only 5 were in this *qada'*, all substandard (YARG 1983*b*:256).[7] These official records, although limited, support the claims of the Jibal Rayma residents that, in comparison to other regions in the governorate, they have received a disproportionately small amount of development assistance.

The evidence indicates that in the governorates with a Zaydi majority, such as Sana^ca and Dhamar, the Shafi^ci minority areas did not fare as well in the competition for scarce development resources. It is highly likely that sectarian discrimination, long part of Yemeni history, played some role in the asymmetrical distribution of central government assistance, but attention should also be given to the organizational abilities of each of the *qada'*s to lobby for this aid.

The internal weakness of the LDA in Jibal Rayma is another factor that may account for the low levels of central government support. The relative gains that the Zaydi areas made may also be viewed as a consequence of unrealized development assistance. Shafi^ci Jibal Rayma, due to its factionalized situation, lacked the internal organizational ability to compete effectively with other regions within the governorate for the central government assistance. Furthermore, as we saw in the review of the LDA leadership, Anis had a large number of "native sons" placed in strategic positions within the central government. In sum, the asymmetrical distribution of development assistance in the western central highlands must be viewed as the result of the combination of these multiple factors.

The National Level

Since the revolution of 1962, the potential for serious national-level sectarian tensions between the northern Zaydi regions of Yemen and the predominantly Shafi^ci south has been greatly reduced. To a large extent, this has been due to the adoption of a more or less informal system of power sharing in the central government. Stookey (1978) reports that the first cabinet of the republic was split almost evenly between Zaydis and Shafi^cis, but notes that the situation did not last long and that during most of the civil war period the influential government posts were held by the Zaydis.

However, in the period of national reconciliation, and especially since the al-Hamdi presidency (1974–78), there has been more equitable power sharing. Since that time, the presidency has been held by a Zaydi and the position of prime minister by a Shafi'i, with the other ministerial posts being assigned primarily according to technical qualifications and expertise. Consequently, the sectarian tensions, so long a feature of Yemeni political life at the national level, have been greatly reduced. As far as this situation may have influenced local development, examination of the official records for education and health actually indicate that in the Shafi'i governorates there are more facilities and services than in the Zaydi north (YARG 1983b: 212, 236–37). It has also often been noted that the Shafi'i south is much more developed economically (Halliday 1974; Stookey 1978). In short, when considering equity in the distribution of central government resources for development, sectarian politics has not been a major issue on the national level.

CONCLUSION

Two different perspectives on the effect of vertical ties such as sectarian alliances on development were referred to in chapter 1. A common argument is that sectarianism is an impediment to national unity and provides a rationale for the asymmetrical distribution of political power, resources, and development programs (Hudson 1968; Barakat 1977). However, the evidence from Yemen suggests that there is a Janus quality to traditional sociopolitical organizations that emerges when analysis is shifted from the local to the regional and national level. When the divisions of tribe or sect are examined at the local level, they are integrative and contribute to the formation of a sense of corporateness that is useful for rural development. When the focus is shifted to a regional level, these same groups take on the appearance of large corporate factions that are in opposition and competition, inhibiting the kinds of wide-scale cooperation seen by some analysts as necessary for rural development. On the national level, these types of groups do not seem to be of much importance at all.

At the village level, sect — due to the fact of religious homogeneity — was basically irrelevant as far as development per se is concerned. If any generalization at all could be entertained, it is that the uniformity in sect affiliation within the village can be seen as a common social denominator and, thus, a facilitator of local development.

At the regional level, tribes and sects have different effects, but they are really only significant in those situations, such as in Sana'a and Dhamar governorates, where tribes and nontribal areas with different sect affiliations compete with each other for development assistance within one administrative system. At this level, central government penetration is still relatively weak, and traditional political oppositions and tensions are still important in regional affairs. Even during the earlier imamic period, centralized authority and the ability to impose policy were regionally variable, and the situation is pretty much as it always has been. Strong tribes have greater political voice than the less integrated tribal areas and, as a result, have been able to direct or channel more of those resources for development that are administered at the governorate level into their own areas. It also should be noted that here there is an overlap between sect and tribe—the strong tribes have been Zaydi and the nontribal regions have been Shafiᶜi. Tribal differences and sectarian differences therefore are combined factors in regional politics. Where there is competition for limited outside resources, advantage has gone to the associations, like Anis, which are part of the power-holding majority. At the level of regional sociopolitical organization, traditional vertical types of social groups were dysfunctional in that the nontribal, sectarian minority areas, such as Jibal Rayma, were unable to compete effectively with the tribal, sectarian majority regions for development assistance, thus impairing their ability to pursue local development.

The social, economic, and political changes in Yemen since the revolution have reduced the importance of tribe and sect at the national level. Political stratification, power sharing, and national integration have progressed to the point that the former condition of northern Zaydi domination over the Shafiᶜi south is now in the past (Zabara 1982:110). The tribes of the north and the nontribal south are gradually being integrated in an expanding central government (Stookey 1978:286). With the majority of development activity being locally generated, the prevailing circumstances may in fact favor development in the south due to better local civil organization, environment, agricultural potential, and commercial networks.

To understand the impact of traditional sociopolitical organizations and social divisions on development, both actual and potential, it is also necessary to analyze them in relation to the style and development strategies in the society. Many of the previous arguments on development have evaluated the effects of traditional organizations in situations where most development is carried out within a centralized, hierarchical system. This strategy is commonly referred to as development from above (Pitt 1976*a*). Under such circumstances (Lebanon is the primary example cited), the potential for problems is increased by the presence of traditional groups locked in competition for development resources, especially when the central government is perceived as weak and its officials as corruptible. In the Yemeni case, only a portion of development resources come from above. These were the outside resources such as financial aid, technical advice, equipment, and staff administered through the ministries, CYDA, and their governorate branch offices. The basic development strategy in Yemen is to utilize locally generated resources, under local control, to meet development needs. Development in Yemen is a mix of limited assistance from above and resources generated from below.

Such a development style shifts the focus of attention away from the centralized system and toward the local associations and local social organizations. The arena in which competition between traditional groups had the greatest impact on local development in the western central highlands was centrally administered outside resources — roughly only one-third of the total resources. Furthermore, this situation has real significance only at the regional level, where there were traditional tribal and sectarian social cleavages. Consequently, the negative aspects of vertical organizations outlined by Barakat (1977) have not reached nearly the proportions in the western central highlands of Yemen that they have in other areas of the Middle East.

8

Conclusion: Lessons Learned

The main objective of this book has been to explore the different experiences in rural development in the western central highlands of the Yemen Arab Republic. Examination of ecological, economic, historical, and sociopolitical variables reveals similarities and differences between Anis and Jibal Rayma. The most important lesson to be drawn from this study is the enormous intracultural and intraregional variation that must be considered when analyzing and planning for rural development. Among the most significant differences discovered are the contrasting constellations of power in the two regions and the variance in sociopolitical structure, most notably in the institution of the tribe (*qabila*) and religious sect.

At the local level, the traditional institution of the tribe has historically demonstrated a potential for occasional corporate action in Anis. Moreover, the tribe provided an ideological basis for uniting the competing interests of social groups spread over a wide area. As a consequence, Anis was better adapted to meet the organizational criteria for the successful functioning of the local development association. Additionally, the tribal institutions have contributed to the success of the Anis LDA by mediating the divisive effects of the atomistic state of social affairs characteristic of most peasant societies (cf. Wolf 1966; Foster 1973). In Jibal Rayma, the opposite obtained. Lacking the mediating and unifying effects of the tribal structure and the accompanying ideology of common relations, the internal cooperation necessary for a successful local development association was even more difficult to achieve and sustain.

In the western central highlands region, traditional sectarian politics was most problematic at the level of intergovernorate politics.

The allocation of central governorate resources for local development was planned and negotiated by committees and offices (i.e., *majlis it-tansiq*, ministerial extension offices) that formed part of the governorate administration. In the governorates of Dhamar and Sana͑a, where one sect was a powerful majority and the other sect a weak minority, the distribution of development assistance was skewed in favor of the dominant sect. Consequently, Anis, as a part of the sectarian majority in the governorate of Dhamar, benefited from this position of power. Jibal Rayma was among the sectarian minorities in Sana͑a governorate and thus in a less advantageous position to obtain development assistance administered at the governorate level.

While the sect and the tribe have been significant forces behind the success of the LDAs in meeting the needs for infrastructure building in the western central highlands of Yemen, they clearly were not the only factors. Economic, geographical, educational, and historical influences were also of importance. By employing a comparative methodology, it has been possible to hold constant some of the underlying economic and ecological factors, thereby enabling a sharper focus and clearer analysis of the role of sociopolitical forces in local development. Although it is beyond the scope of this work to try and establish relative weights for each of these factors, the analysis has succeeded in describing how they operated in the development process in the western central highlands.

Finally, the relations of power in Jibal Ramya and Anis were quite different, particularly after the revolution. In Jibal Rayma, an elite class had been stripped of a large proportion of its livelihood and political legitimacy; in the power vacuum created by the revolution, it tried to regain some of its lost power by controlling the local resources of the LDA. It was challenged by the emerging local class of young professionals and the politically astute. The conflict that ensued retarded development. In Anis, no significant shifts in power were triggered by the revolution; as a consequence, conflict was limited and local development proceeded at a faster pace.

In addition to the empirical problem of local development, this book has sought to shed some light on the more general issues of social change in peasant society and to address the question of whether or not vertical organizations are necessarily dysfunctional for socio-economic development and change. The former imamic regime, the main source of what could be termed "oppression," was overthrown in 1962 by a military coup d'etat, thus opening the door for economic and social change. The result, at the local level, has been the partial transformation from the "nonproductive" peasant economy of prerevolutionary times to a more mixed farming/small business rural economy. This was largely a consequence of the improved internal political climate coupled with the large-scale cash inputs from temporary migration to the neighboring oil-producing states.

While the prerevolutionary peasant economy is now approaching a farming/mercantile economy, there is continuity within change. Land tenure patterns are not undergoing radical transformation. Most people in the western central highlands own some land and still use it to produce the traditional cereal crops for household consumption. Those fortunate to control land suited for qat or other cash crops produce them for the developing market. Thus, the peasant farming aspect of Yemeni society characterized by a majority of small landowners/producers is continuing in the rural highlands.

The local development movement occurred within the traditional sociopolitical framework. Yemen is a good example of how social change may be initiated from within and motivated from below. The Yemen local development movement also provides evidence that challenges the common assertions that vertical sociopolitical organizations are inherently dysfunctional for development. In the case presented here, the tribe clearly was an asset and was adaptable enough to meet the requirements of the modern cooperative. The tribe not only provided an ideological basis for integrating what little assistance came from above, but also offered significant precedent for community organization. Far from being a barrier to change, the tribe was a facilitator of change. In the Yemen example of local development, the form of infrastructure building carried out under the auspices of the local development association showed how a traditional organization can be positively associated with rural development.

Although it has been argued here that traditional forms of sociopolitical organization may be a positive organizing vehicle for rural development, I do not mean to argue that they are a prerequisite for success. Traditional organizations such as the tribe may provide the necessary ideological basis for cooperation, but this can also be achieved by the development of class consciousness and other secular ideologies. The southern areas of Yemen have a more civil form of community identification, based on the ideas of territory and community. Subdistricts in this region have developed a generalized sense of corporate identity, formed associations for local development, and completed some of the first LDA projects. The LDA experience in Yemen demonstrates that associations can be successful in a variety of social contexts, either tribal or secular (territorial, community-based), so long as they provide the social basis for forming and maintaining a corporate group (e.g., an LDA).

A common problem facing the anthropologist is the limitation of the case study method in the development of general propositions. In this book, an additional objective has been to provide a case study of local development that might contribute toward the generation of "grounded" development theory and the formation of new development paradigms and to suggest ways that the Yemen materials may be useful for development administrators and planners in the Middle East.[1] The Yemen case suggests that in situations where development is principally motivated from below, social institutions can be successfully adapted into more formal corporate entities to implement local rural development projects.

Judgments concerning the usefulness of traditional organizations and whether or not they should be included or left out of development plans should be based on careful consideration of the type of development activity planned as well as the type of traditional organization. For example, recent development studies have pointed to many cases where the potential for traditional organizations to be positively associated with rural development is clearly limited. Haaland (1980), in a review of the problems of development in the savannah regions of Sudan, demonstrates the difficulties of utilizing traditional administrative units for organizing development activities. As a result of the British colonial administration, the correlation leadership, tribal structure, and territory no longer exists (Haaland 1980:67). Under such circumstances, the social structure has been so altered as to make it inappropriate as a vehicle for enhancing corporate action or rural development. Nevertheless, one can also find case examples from other areas in the Middle East where the traditional organization has been positively integrated into development schemes (see Cantori and Harik 1984; Khadr 1984:92).

When examined from a cross-cultural perspective, the evidence either to support or to refute the notion that vertical organizations such as tribes are a good social base for development is inconclusive. In fact, contradictory hypotheses can be found in the literature. For example, in a study of the Ethiopian local development associations (*mahabar*), Hamer argues that kinship heterogeneity and competition between groups are structural prerequisites for successful local development associations (1976:118–119). On the other hand, in an overview of indigenous organizations, Saunders (cited in Cohen et al. 1981:1051) argues that they are likely to have more success in rural development if the population in the area is socially cohesive, if there has been a traditional basis for cooperative action, and if kinship organization can be involved in forming the collectives. Clearly, the question is still open.

In a cross-cultural study of 150 local organizations involved in rural development, Esman and Uphoff have examined the relationship between local organization performance and a set of physical and social environmental variables. These variables (many of which parallel those examined in this study) include topography, resource endowment, income levels, social stratification, group patterns, and community and societal norms. Esman and Uphoff could find no statistical relationship, either positive or negative, between local organization performance (i.e., successful or unsuccessful) and these antecedent variables (1984:103–122). Their results are surprising in that they run against much of the conventional wisdom regarding the interplay of environment and social institutions. The results of their hologeistic study point out a basic problem in development research: environmental variables "are not constant in their effect; that is that the effects they have can work in either direction" (Esman and Uphoff 1984:125). Depending on the circumstances, environmental variables (both physical and social) can have positive, neutral, or negative effects on the performance of local organizations in rural development. The explanation Esman and Uphoff offer for their inconclusive findings is that when cross-cultural comparisons are made, the respective opposite relationships statistically offset each other.

The Yemen case may resolve some of the confusion inherent in this analysis by suggesting certain other criteria that should be taken into consideration in the cross-cultural study of local organizations and development. Along with differentiating local organizations according to their general functions (i.e., credit associations, local development associations, and cooperatives) as Esman and Uphoff did, it seems critical to distinguish between the types of development activity and criteria for membership in the development organization. This is important because, as Esman and Uphoff point out, local development organizations are frequently unsuccessful due to: (1) *resistance* of either the population or the central government to their formation; (2) *subordination*, that is, losing local autonomy and being taken over by outside interests; (3) *internal divisions*; and (4) *ineffectiveness and malpractice* (1984:181). These types of problems are often inherent in the very structure of the local organizations and may be obviated through selective modifications. The success of the Yemen cases suggests some principles of organization that may reduce these types of problems.

In the Yemen model, local development activities are in the public domain and are concentrated on infrastructure building. Membership and access to benefits from LDA activities are "automatically" shared among a general membership that is determined by residence — that is, there are no other specific requirements for general membership in the association. No specific joining fees are required as they are, for example, in production-oriented cooperatives.[2] One of the consequences of this type of association is that the individual member does not expect a calculated return from the association based on contribution. In this sense, membership may be conceived of as being passive. The LDA is the collectivity of all the residents whose tax money is used for the improvement of their locality. With passive membership, there are fewer chances for the development of tensions between members and nonmembers, reducing the potential for local resistance to the association. Second, the goals of the Yemeni local development associations are directed toward community needs, rather than the needs of specific individuals. Where other forms of local development organizations, such as cooperatives and credit associations, are specifically designed as income-generating activities to benefit a limited, selective membership (and thus may be conceived of as individual-oriented),[3] the Yemeni LDAs are specifically community-oriented. Consequently, there are fewer tensions between the development organization and its general membership than there would be if there were expectations for direct individual return on the investments. Projects designed to benefit the community rather than individual members may reduce the potential for malpractice, graft, favoritism, and malfeasance, which have plagued other cooperative movements in the developing world. In the Yemen model, occasional corruption resulting from, for example, the forging of receipts does occur, but it is limited in scope because of built-in community auditing measures that make it difficult for leadership to divert large sums of the tax revenues for personal gain. The possibility for subordination is reduced in LDAs like the Yemen example precisely because they are community-oriented. To explore this point, we may contrast the example of the Egyptian Aswan Fishing Cooperative. This cooperative, while not exactly successful in implementing a policy of increasing equality among the workers, was a financial success, and the members were making such a profit that the Egyptian government formed a secondary company that controlled transportation of the production of the fishermen, undermining the original cooperative and effectively subordinating the Aswan association (Khadr 1984). Community-based cooperatives such as the Yemeni LDAs, with a focus on infrastructure building rather than profit, are less attractive for takeover by outside interests.

A third important factor that must be considered in examining the structure of development associations is financing. The Yemeni associations have multisource financing. General operating expenses and one-third of the project financing comes from *zakat*. This ancient Islamic tax has been a part of the Yemeni social system at least since the inception of the Zaydi nearly a thousand years ago. Consequently, financing for the general operation of the LDA does not come in the form of an additional financial burden above basic traditional taxes. Instead of all tax revenues leaving the rural areas, in Yemen locally generated funds remain where their benefits can be seen. Only when projects are approved by the various levels of government are any additional direct contributions requested from the people, most often in the form of labor and materials. Because the development association is dealing with public tax revenues, the LDA budget is under the scrutiny of the village secretaries. As the rather protracted case of Jibal Rayma shows, although accusations can be made, there is really not much potential for gross levels of malfeasance because of the necessity for public accountability. In sum, locally generated revenues stay within the community in a straightforward system; the Yemen system requires accountability and benefits can be directly seen. Only the central government portion of the financing system is open to local question and criticism. The central government portion of the financing is problematic because it is administered through governorate offices, where political considerations are often more important than felt needs.

The Yemen model of financing local development contrasts with other direct contribution systems in which a special outlay of cash or capital is required for membership. Under direct financing schemes, such as credit associations and production-oriented cooperatives, there is a great potential for financial malfeasance and control by politically powerful groups or individuals (see, for example, Bryant and White 1982:290; Morss and Gow 1985).

Finally, the Yemeni LDA is organized in a hierarchical manner, with multiple levels of authority and control; checks and balances are built into the system, and there are internal policing mechanisms. This corresponds to one of the few significant positive correlations that Esman and Uphoff report for successful local development organizations (1984:150–155). The Yemen LDA model has local, governorate, and national levels of organization. The power of CYDA to levy and enforce sanctions through its judicial branch reduces the potential for corruption. Although it is doubtful that any system is completely effective in eliminating malfeasance, the Yemen system makes a reasonable effort. Additionally, the LDAs maintain planning departments at the national level with a professional staff (e.g., accountants, engineers, lawyers) who oversee local projects and supervise and approve plans. This also reduces the problem of ineffectiveness.

The experience of the Yemeni LDAs suggests that these four criteria — community-directed goals, passive membership, multiple financing using existing tax structure, and hierarchical institutional formalization with checks and balances — could be effectively used to differentiate between various types of local development organizations. The Yemen case suggests that, where the above criteria are met, traditional corporate groups, such as the tribe, may be useful vehicles to organize local development activities.

If a development paradigm is to be useful, it should facilitate the replication of successes and minimize the repetition of failures. This study has focused on the analysis of sociopolitical and organizational aspects of society that have been associated with both success and failure in local development. The Yemen model for rural development may be appropriate and potentially applicable in other areas of the Middle East to the extent that there are (1) similar cultural patterns and values; (2) perceived needs for infrastructure building; and (3) comparable financial institutions (especially the Islamic *zakat*). It appears less applicable where there are major differences in historical experience, particularly where the colonial experience has affected traditional social organization. Even under such conditions, however, some of the "bottom up" development activities could be effective; but this must be determined by detailed situational analysis of the prevailing sociopolitical, economic, and cultural conditions.

Finally, I would like to speculate on the future of rural development in the western central highlands. So long as the economic situation in the Arabian Peninsula continues to afford the opportunity for high remittances to expatriate Yemeni workers, the local development associations can continue to benefit from control of the *zakat* revenues and direct contributions. If the regional economic situation changes, the central government may be forced to take a larger percentage of the *zakat*, which would have a damaging effect on the associations.

Anis has a well-established LDA administration and organization, and the three *nahiya* associations continue to share office space and facilities in Sana ͨa; they will, in my estimation, continue to operate successfully, especially since they are actively involved in reconstruction activities as a consequence of the 1982 earthquake.

The future for Jibal Rayma will probably be brighter than the recent past. Political tensions in the area have dissipated to a large extent, and some of the local leaders who were very active in the confrontations over LDA power are no longer on the political scene. As economic conditions and education improve, and the state infrastructure replaces the remnants of the *ancient régime*, the LDA will become less susceptible to conflict. Jibal Rayma is moving in this direction. Additionally, as other regions in Yemen continue to make progress, it is highly likely that their successes will influence Jibal Rayma, which will then emulate the more productive cooperatives.

Notes

1. INTRODUCTION

1. The number of LDAs increased from 29 in 1973 to well over 124 in the course of two years. This has been attributed to the active encouragement of President al-Hamdi who, as a former head of CYDA, used the LDA movement to promote his political career. See Carapico (1984) for the most detailed discussion of the political economy and history of the Yemen local development movement.

2. The concept of a paradigm, as usually explained in social science, refers to a body of scientific theory used for analysis of problems (Kuhn 1970). In development literature, the term is sometimes used to refer to a development strategy (e.g., Stohr and Taylor 1981), and sometimes to refer to the body of development theory (Foster-Carter 1976). One cannot speak of development from below as a scientific paradigm, yet it is possible to speak of the need to develop a paradigm by which development from below can be explained. It is this sense of the term that is implied in this study.

3. Carapico (1984) characterizes the Yemen movement as a "middle-both ways" type system, which is similar to the perspective offered in this book.

4. For a fuller discussion of the important situational studies of development, see Pitt (1976*b*). A more general discussion of the concept of social situations is found in Garbett (1970).

5. See Pelto (1970:6) and Lengyel (1971:214) for discussions and examples of holistic research in anthropology.

6. Qat, *Catha edulis*, is a stimulant widely chewed by the Yemenis in a wide variety of social events.

2. HUMAN ECOLOGY

1. Revri (1983) defines the following climatic zones: (1) coastal Tihama plain with high humidity and low precipitation (0–80 mm), (2) central Tihama plain with lower humidity and irregular low precipitation (0–150 mm), (3) western mountains area near Tihama plains with low to medium precipitation (0–300 mm), (4) lower slopes with low precipitation (200–400 mm), (5) upper mountain slopes with medium rainfall (300–600 mm), (6) western mountainous highlands (research area) with medium to abundant rainfall (200–1,000 mm), (7) central highlands with medium

177

rainfall (200–1,000 mm), (8) eastern mountain slopes with low periodic rainfall (100–400 mm), and (9) eastern desert zones with low rainfall (0–200 mm). Additionally, Steffen et al. (1978) distinguish among Tihama plains, western escarpment, eastern escarpment, southern uplands, central plateau, and eastern desert.

2. Measured at Zabid in central Tihama. The humidity becomes higher as one approaches the coast or the foothills.

3. In a few regions such as Jabal Bura^c and 'Udayn, stands of trees still exist, primarily *Acacia negrii*, *Ziziphus spina-christi*, and local hardwoods, but most trees are scattered among the terraces. Some are planted as symbiotic crops with the coffee for needed shade, especially *tannib* (*Cordia abyssinica*).

4. Chilcote defines peasants as "farmers who do not own their land and are usually associated with precapitalist modes of production, for example, squatters, renters and unpaid family workers" (1984:8). However, by restricting "peasants" to those who have no ownership of land, such a definition effectively cuts off a good portion of the developing world. A more satisfactory definition, and one that is applicable to prerevolutionary Yemen, is offered by Wolf: "Rural cultivators whose surpluses are transferred to a dominant group of rulers that use the surpluses both to underwrite its own standard of living and to distribute the remainder to groups in society that do not farm but must be fed for their specific goods and services in turn" (1966:3–4). Peasants also produce primarily for household consumption, and not directly for an economic market (Redfield 1956:18). The differing feature of Wolf's models of peasant society is that ownership of land is not the real issue, but rather rights to production surpluses—as some kind of lien on the land, either in the form of direct payment to a landlord in the case of sharecropping agreements or in the form of tax.

> The peasant then [was] subject to asymmetrical power relations which made a permanent charge on his production. Such a charge, paid out as the result of some superior claim to his labor on the land, we call rent, regardless of whether that rent is paid in labor, produce or money. Where someone exercises an effective superior power or domain over a cultivator, the cultivator must produce a fund of rent. . . . It is this production of a fund of rent which critically distinguishes the peasant from the primitive cultivator. (Wolf 1966:10)

The Yemeni agricultural producer during the Zaydi dynasties produced primarily for domestic production. Surpluses, beyond the need for household maintenance, were extracted from the rural areas in the form of taxes imposed by the Zaydi state and collected by appointed tax farmers who often bought the privilege (Halliday 1974; Kennedy, personal communication). Consequently, there was no direct production for a nonlocal market, and there was a permanent lien on agricultural supplies in the form of taxation. Thus, the society satisfied the economic requirements to classify it as peasant.

5. Gross economic statistics are not very reliable. Cohen and Lewis (1979a) report estimates between 40 and 70 percent. The 1983 statistical yearbook breaks down the GDP by sectors; excluding the government services sector, agriculture accounts for about 35 percent. Previously, the only mineral export from Yemen was salt. In the late seventies and early eighties, cement production has expanded, but mostly for domestic consumption. Hunt Oil Company, an American firm, struck oil in the desert region near Ma^{c}rib in July 1984 and has drilled twenty-five successful wells. A refinery has been built near the fields; estimates suggest that as much as 60 percent of domestic needs may be filled.

6. Average sizes of hamlets were calculated for Jibal Rayma and Anis based on the 1981 CYDA census. The average was determined by counting the number of hamlets and dividing by the number of families in the *qaḍa*'s. The Swiss Technical Cooperation (1977) study of household density sets the average number of families per household at one.

3. PATTERNS OF RURAL DEVELOPMENT

1. The assertion by Cohen and Lewis (1979a) that Yemen manifests the condition of a capital surplus/labor short economy requires some comment. It is unclear from their discussion precisely what is meant by capital surplus. If by "capital" they mean the standard definition of a country's stock of man-made means of production (i.e., buildings, factories, machinery, tools, equipment) and current inventory of produced goods, it is not accurate to state that Yemen has a capital surplus. One does not find farm equipment lying idle; in fact, the few factories in Yemen are either in production or broken down due to obsolete technology and lack of spare parts (e.g., the "Chinese" textile factory in Sanaᶜa). Yet there appear to be enormous amounts of cash available for investment that could be converted into productive capital. If Cohen and Lewis mean by the term the tremendous flow of liquid assets, particularly the cash generated through expatriate remittances, then it is possible to accept their argument for a capital surplus. It is important to demonstrate that this condition exists to support or refute their claim that there is no shortage of cash in the system and to establish the fact that Yemen is in fact not a "poor" country despite the evidence presented in its national accounts.

2. As part of an extended family unit that owned a farm, and having a brother who owned a successful tailor shop, this person supplemented his earnings by settling disputes in the region, for which he received a considerable compensation.

3. The money supply for Yemen 1982 was 12,519.4 million rials. Of this 8,940.5, or 71 percent, was currency outside of banks. Only 24.2 percent was in banks in the form of demand, time, or savings deposits (YARG 1983b:193).

4. The evidence given here indicates a very high rate of inflation in the Yemeni economy, but it should be remembered that the Yemeni rial was tied to the U.S. dollar (4.54 rials = $1. U.S.). Inflation, therefore, was not due to devalued currency, but instead was due to a large money supply chasing after few goods and services, driving prices upward. Additionally, increased dependence on foreign goods has caused some prices to rise.

5. Private bank transfers in millions of U.S. dollars by year: 1973, 132; 1974, 225; 1975, 525; 1976, 1,013; 1977, 1,411; 1978, 1,243; 1979, 1,359; 1980, 1,096; 1981, 987 (source: YARG 1983b:186).

6. For a more detailed description, see Cohen et al. 1980.

7. I have written this account in the past tense because law number 12 of 1985 and the accompanying explanatory note number 83, also of 1985, have significantly altered the structure and functioning of the Yemeni local development associations. The stated purposes of these changes are better coordination of the local development association activities with the activities of the line ministries and greater centralization and planning of rural development. In order to accomplish these general goals, specific changes have been made. The new law mandates the reorganization of the previous LDAs (generally called *taᶜawaniyat*) into newly structured local development associations (*al-majalis al-mahalliya lil tatwir at- taᶜawuni*). These associations are to work in tandem with the newly created district (*nahiya*) executive coun-

cil (*majlis it-tanfidh*) in planning local development. The *majlis it-tanfidh* is composed of officials such as the director (*mudir*) of the *nahiya*, director of finances, director of schools, director of health, and other representatives of the central government, including the district representative to the permanent people's conference (*lajna da'iyma lil mu͑tamir ash-sha͑bi*). In many areas, the *nahiya majlis it-tansiq* replaces the former municipal council (*majlis ib-baladiya*).

Under the new organization, a new public administration entity also called the coordinating council (*majlis it-tansiq*) has been organized at the district (*nahiya*) level that is made up of the officers of the LDA administrative committee (*hai'a id-dariya*) and the district executive committee (*majlis it-tanfidh*). Consequently, much of the work that was done at the governorate level is now to be done at the district level.

The new LDA structure is similar to the former in that it still maintains local, governorate, and national levels of organization and the election of delegates to the general assembly. At the local level, candidates for membership in the LDA are still elected as members of the general assembly by popular vote. However, there are significant differences. The number of members is now determined according to population based on the formula of 1 representative for each 500 residents. In the 1985 election, 17,951 members were elected to the general assembly. Each district LDA general assembly elects an administrative board (*hai'a id-dariya*). The administrative board includes the offices of chairman, general secretary, and treasurer and, depending on the size of the *nahiya*, may consist of between 7 and 12 members.

Coordination and planning of LDA activities at the governorate level are still under the auspices of the coordinating council (*majlis it-tansiq*) but it is now a regional branch office of the General Secretariat of the *majalis al-mahalliya*. Much of the work previously done at the national headquarters of CYDA in Sana͑a will now be done at the governorate branch office.

At the national level, the general assembly is presided over by the president of the republic and is composed of the presidents and at least three other members of the administrative boards from each *nahiya* LDA. The general assembly is overseen by the administrative committee, which consists of the president of the republic, minister of development and head of the Central Planning Organization (CPO), interior minister, finance minister, head of the Central Auditing Agency, and deputy ministers for education, health, housing, social welfare, public works, electricity, water, transportation, *waqf*, and information. Additionally, the administrative committee contains twenty-two members elected from the general assembly, two from each governorate. Of the two officers from each governorate, one is stationed in the general offices in Sana͑a and the other in the branch office located in the governorate capital. It is hoped that, by having one of the members of the general assembly of the *majalis al-mahalliya* stationed in each of the governorate branch offices and the other in Sana͑a, the needs of the local communities will be served in a more efficient manner.

The General Secretariat of the *majalis al-mahalliya lil tatwir at-ta͑awuni* (formerly CYDA) now consists of the secretary general, assistant secretary, and nine departments. The planning and statistics, legal, and public relations departments and office of the general secretary are under the stewardship of the secretary general; the departments of local and regional committees, inspection and auditing, research, services, and production are the responsibility of the assistant secretary general. The planning and administrative functions of the General Secretariat continue to be similar to the former CYDA; however, the national general assembly has a greater involvement in the allocation of financial resources.

All LDAs are now obliged to develop one-year and five-year master plans in conjunction with the other offices in the district. The plans are to be submitted to the governorate branch office and then sent to the General Secretariat under the signature of the governor. In the General Secretariat they are reviewed by the various technical departments and, once approved, sent to the Central Planning Organization (CPO) of the prime minister's office. This is to ensure that the CPO, which is responsible for all facets of development and economic planning in the republic, is aware of the LDA projects and that they are in alignment with the Yemen government five-year plan.

Once LDA plans are approved by CPO and the relevant ministries, they then face a general review by the administrative committee of the general assembly and a vote of approval. After passing this stage, the LDA receives the funding for its projects. Final allocation and approval of projects are assigned a priority according to the needs of the community. Three criteria are important: population, needs of the district, and if it is one of the *majalis al-mahalliya* "special projects." These factors have been proposed in order to redress some of the unequal development that occurred over the first decade of operations. In order to receive a high priority, the project must serve a large population that will derive important benefit from its implementation. Areas where there has been little development or slow growth and, consequently, a greater need receive higher priority. Additionally, the *majalis al-mahalliya* have some independent funds from outside agencies that are used to finance their own high-priority special projects.

Significant changes have been made in the area of finance. Previously, each chartered local development association was entitled to up to 75 percent of the *zakat*. The tax was assessed and collected by deputies, either the community secretaries (*ᶜumana*) or local shaykhs, who transferred it to the *nahiya* director of finance (*mudir al-mal*). The *zakat* revenues were divided at the district office; only one-quarter was transferred to the Ministry of Finance. The LDA received its share directly from the *nahiya* financial office and deposited it directly into the LDA bank accounts. Thus, collection and disbursement of funds was largely a local affair under the control of the local development board and there was a degree of local autonomy in financial affairs of the LDA.

Under the revised system, all *zakat* taxes are transferred from the district financial office to the Ministry of Finance, where they are pooled together in a central national local development association budget and then allocated to projects according to the priorities set by the *majalis al-mahalliya*.

8. There was some dispute over this man's claim as shaykh.

4. CONTRAST IN DEVELOPMENT: JIBAL RAYMA AND ANIS

1. Estimates calculated from examination of 1:50,000 contour maps (Directorate of Overseas Surveys, United Kingdom 1979).

2. It should be noted that the trend in road building is to cut a crude access road and keep extending it, despite severe damage caused by the tropical rains. In the initial states, repair is only enough to keep the road passable. Exceptions are roads considered to be of immediate strategic value.

3. Estimate provided by the director of schools in Dawran Anis.

4. The health center of Jabal ish-Shirq is actually in Madinat ish-Shirq, due to its central location, and al-Juma^c has a subcenter supported by the LDA, the Ministry of Health, and the private practice of a local doctor. In no rural health center visited in Yemen could services be considered full, but they do function and provide limited care and, considering the circumstances, do an adequate job.

5. The time frame of this study is roughly from 1972 to 1982 in Anis and 1973 to 1983 in Jibal Rayma.

6. There was a small contingent of expatriates assigned to the Madinat ish-Shirq center in 1978, but the program was very short-lived.

7. Carapico argues that North Yemen was a peripheral capitalist state until the recent decades. Too often the history of North Yemen is lumped with that of the south, and its integration into the world economic system is overly stressed. Clearly, Yemen was not totally isolated, but at the local level the effects of the outside system were limited.

8. For an excellent discussion of the narrow world view of the people who live in isolated mountain communities, see Morris (1985). Morris's field work was conducted during the same time in a western mountain community two ranges to the north with similar ecological conditions.

9. For example, contracts for the health center in Hammam ʿAli, Anis, were negotiated in 1979, and the entire building was completed in 1982. Likewise, the schools in Bayt al-ʿAkwa and Bani Fadl were negotiated at the same time and also completed in 1982. The Anis road project was completed in about three years and is over ninety kilometers in length.

10. These estimates were obtained by multiplying the area under production (hectares) by the gross-margin to obtain the total revenue theoretically generated. Agricultural tax is levied at between 5 and 10 percent, depending on whether the land is irrigated or not. For a conservative estimate, the lower tax rate of 5 percent (irrigated lands) was used for coffee and 10 percent for grain. Data are based on Revri's (1983) analysis of aerial photographs.

11. Of course, area under production is not necessarily the same as actual realized production. In many areas, such as the Maʿbar/Jahran plains, high winds, poor soil quality, and occasional frost may severely affect yields. Likewise, higher yields may be expected in the lower elevations such as the western slopes of Jibal Rayma where there is better rainfall and more moderate temperatures. The yields of areas under production are based on a national average calculated by Revri (1983) and are only approximations; but, in the absence of agricultural census data with specific yield measurements, it is the best estimate possible at this time.

12. Kennedy (1987:157) reports that there is also supposed to be a 10 percent field tax on qat, but it is uncertain if this would be considered *zakat* and therefore potential LDA revenue. I have opted to omit this from my calculations, although it would undoubtedly raise the revenue-generating ability of Jibal Rayma significantly.

13. Anis LDA provided me with a detailed budget for the year 1978–79. The Rayma LDA, being in the throes of much turmoil, with a budget being investigated for possible malfeasance, would not release the figures. However, a number of informants closely involved in the association reported that in 1978–79 the budget was around 2 million rials, and I am confident of their accuracy.

5. SOCIAL ORGANIZATION AND POWER

1. See Peters (1967) for a discussion of African Bedouin social organization and the processes of genealogical telescoping.

2. See Dresch (1984) for a discussion of the types of power the paramount shaykh may wield.

3. See Adra (1982) for a fuller discussion of the notion of what it means to be a tribesman.

4. Dresch (1986) rightly argues that the supposed massing effect of the tribes is rare and by no means automatic. However, I also recall how a co-worker, a repatriated Yemeni born in Ethiopia, expressed fear and caution when encountering a stranger in a gas station who was from a tribe near his. He explained to me that there was some kind of feud going on between the tribes; even though he was socially very far removed from the situation, he felt he might be shot as part of the feud. Events play a big part, but the ideology is still present.

5. For a fuller discussion of tribal organization, see Dresch (1984) and Adra (1982). In the western central highlands, the tribal structure is considerably weaker than in the places reported in these studies and is in eclipse in many areas.

6. Chelhod (1970) seems to merge the lineage system with the tribal system when he argues that *qabila* designates the tribe and *batn* and *fakhdh* are its two main divisions. My evidence indicates that these are terms used to refer to lineage and not tribal structure.

7. *Habl* seems to be confined to the north and was not used in Anis or Jibal Rayma. Its importance in Stevenson's analysis may be due to the fact that he analyzed a town situation and not a rural farming area.

8. See Chelhod (1970:85–86) for a list of the major tribes of the Hashid and Bakil federations.

9. It should be noted that this problem emerged after the breakup of the Anis LDA into the three district associations. Under the previous structure, problems like the road alignments could be negotiated by the planning committee before things got out of hand.

10. ʿUtama is one of the few districts that is situated in the buffer zone between the two major sects and is roughly half Zaydi and half Shafiʿi. It is a good example of a transitional area in which the local sociopolitical organization begins to shift from the highland tribal model to the western central highlands variation. This district is organized into five *mikhlaf*s—as-Samah, Himyar, Bani Bahr, Sumal, and Razih. Unlike neighboring Anis, which considers the *mikhlaf*s tribal segments, in ʿUtama the *mikhlaf*s are referred to as territorial divisions, "sides of the mountain." In contrast, the five nominally Bakili tribes in ʿUtama—Bani as-Samawi, Bani al-Maʿalami, Bani al-Ghabiri, Bani al-Muhsin, and Bani al-Maʾazabi—do not correspond exactly to these territorial divisions. Additionally, in ʿUtama there are a few other groups—often referred to as tribes—that, in a manner resembling the western central highlands mode of organization, trace their ancestry directly to other areas. For example, the Bayt al-Buʿathi, Bayt al-Muhsin ad-Dakhali, and Bayt al-Muhsin al-Kharaji are from Bani Matar and the Bayt al-Muqaddam are from Jahran.

11. *Nahiya* Dawran has thirty-one *ʿuzla*s, *nahiya* Jabal ish-Shirq has twenty-two, and *nahiya* Maʿbar/Jahran is divided into four.

12. Compare this, for example, with the office of paramount shaykh among the Hashid, where Bayt al-Ahmar has held the office for generations (Dresch 1984:31–48).

13. It should be pointed out that a third category of people in the prerevolutionary power structure were a few large coffee merchants, who also had considerable economic wealth. However, these families were mostly in al-Jabin, in an area near where a British health development team was working. I was warned that I would be reported to the government as a "spy" by the team leader if I ventured into this area, so I must apologize for the lack of data on this category.

14. For example, Jon Bjørnsson (personal communication), a socially perceptive architect who worked in Wasab al-ᶜAli, the next mountain range to the south of Jibal Rayma, reports that there was a class of very powerful landlords who owned extremely large tracts of land with many tenant farmers. Tutwiler seems to indicate a similar situation in Mahwit (personal communication).

15. I had the opportunity to live in the town of Manakha for two months doing agricultural survey work for a German development project. During this time, one of the larger coffee merchants explained the difficulty in grading and typing and the problems it caused with foreign buyers.

6. LOCAL POLITICS, CORPORATE GROUPS, AND DEVELOPMENT

1. See chapter 5 for discussion of the variable importance of kinship, residence, and political alliance in ascertaining tribal membership.

2. I would like to thank Hydar ᶜAli Nagi for sharing his account of local history.

3. Carapico (1984:177–78) points out that the earliest cooperatives were formed in the port city of al-Hudayda and argues a linkage between the development of the Yemeni system and the capitalist system.

4. I have intentionally obscured the identity of this public figure.

7. IDEOLOGY AND LOCAL DEVELOPMENT

1. See the discussion in Stevenson (1985) on LDA leadership and social status in the ᶜAmran area north of Sanaᶜa.

2. In more recent times, intellectuals involved in the revolution, such as ᶜAbdul Rahman al-Beidhani, also saw the political problems in Yemen just prior to the revolution in sectarian terms. His position was that Yemen was dominated by the Zaydi *sada*, a foreign element that had no rightful position in the Yemeni state. He advocated that Yemen be partitioned into two regions, one Zaydi and the other Shafiᶜi, and that the *sada* have no place in the new state (Zabara 1982:41). Although al-Beidhani's position was not adopted and, in fact, many leaders of the revolution were Zaydi, it does illustrate how sectarian differences have been considered a key political issue.

3. Examination of the alliances of the tribes with either the republican or royalist causes in the 1962–70 revolutionary war suggests a correlation between cause and sect. All of the tribes aligned with the royalists were Zaydi; although some Zaydi tribes were allied with the republicans, all of the Shafiᶜi areas were republican. Although some writers, including Zabara (1982), have cast the Yemeni revolution in terms of a conflict between traditionalists and modernists, it is difficult to ignore the importance of sectarian differences and the fact that most Shafiᶜis considered themselves to be politically dominated by the Zaydi elites.

4. Another example of how political conflicts were conveniently categorized in sectarian terms was the attempt of an important local leader, in 1978, to lead a part

of the Hujjariya (southern YAR) to secede from the republic and join the People's Democratic Republic of Yemen (PDRY). This insurrection was dealt with by sending a militia from the north. When fighting broke out and government troops from the Zaydi north were sent in, the conflict took on the appearance of a sectarian-based dispute. Although the periodic political confrontations in Yemen are complex and cannot simply be reduced to sectarian conflict, it is one of the first rationales used by the people to explain their problems.

5. Zabara (1982) and many progressive young Yemenis interviewed preferred to discount the Zaydi-Shafiᶜi split, arguing that the ideological differences between the two sects are small and no longer an issue in modern Yemen. However, people in Shafiᶜi areas such as Wasab al-ᶜAli and Wasab as-Safil concluded that, among other things, their underdevelopment was due to concentration of assistance in the Zaydi area.

6. This point was clearly explained to me by Muhammad ᶜAbdullah al-Fadli, an influential young organizer in Anis.

7. This is an aggregated figure and includes doctors in Sanaᶜa.

8.CONCLUSION: LESSONS LEARNED

1. See Glasser and Strauss (1967) for a discussion of the generation of grounded theory.

2. Johnston and Clark (1982) provide an excellent discussion of the different requirements for production- versus consumption-oriented rural development. The Yemen local development associations are engaged in what they would classify as consumption-oriented development.

3. The disaggregated list of development organization in Esman and Uphoff's (1984) study is predominantly composed of economic cooperatives where each member invests and expects an individual return. Also, see the case examples in Worsley (1971), which are all this type of cooperative.

Glossary

Singular, Plural	Translation
ʿabid, ʿibad	slave
ʿaql	wise man, local leader
ʿayan	important families
ʿayana	general term for cooperation
akhdam	former servants of the state, pariah group
amin	secretary
badana	lineage
baladi	home-produced, anything native
batn	(literally, stomach) descent group
bayʿa	merchant, seller
bayt, buyut	household, house
da'ima	extended family
dawshan	village crier, go-between, fool
dhimmi	protected, non-Muslim people of the book
diwan	large room used for entertaining guests, living room
diya	blood money
fakhdh	branch of a lineage
faqih, fuqaha	religious adept, healer, mystic
faza	form of cooperation
fish	open tribal lands
futa	skirt, kiltlike dress worn by men
habl	(literally, rope, sinew) genealogical connections
hajar	slaughtering an animal in settlement of a dispute, to obligate someone
hakim	judge in legal courts
himi	open tribal lands
hukuma	government office buildings, seat of rural government

Isma'ili	sect of Shi'a Islam
'izz	honor
ja'ish	traditional agricultural cooperation
jabal, jibal	mountain
jaysh	army
jiwar	protection
jubha	front
khums	one-fifth, a tribal segment typical in Bedouin culture
lahma	(literally, meat) clan
mahal, mahalat	hamlet
mal	finance, capital
mamsa, mamasi	local administrative division, cluster of hamlets
masakin	poor, unfortunate
masha'ikh	the class of leaders, shaykhs
mikhlaf, mikhalif	subdistrict, tribal segment
milk	private property
miri	state-owned lands
mudir	director
mufraj	large room used for entertaining guests, chewing qat, living room, same as *diwan*
mughram, mugharam	subdistrict in Jibal Rayma
musawa'a	equality
mut'allim	educated
mutafanni	experienced
nahiya	district, a government administrative unit
qa'id	military chief
qa'	depression, valley
qabayla	tribal ethos
qabila	tribe
qabili, qaba'il	tribesman
qada	a dry measure, a large gunnysack
qada'	subprovince, major administrative segment of a governorate composed of a number of districts
qadhi, qudha	religious judge or authority, member of traditional elite
qarya, qura	village
qat	*Catha edulis* Forsk., a shrub whose tender leaves are chewed for a mild stimulant effect
rubta	a bundle of qat
rubu'	(literally, a quarter) small section of a tribe
sahi, sahin	nurse
sayyid, sada	descendant of the Prophet

shabab	young men, youth; used to refer to young intellectuals
Shafi°i	sect of Sunni Islam
Shari°a	Islamic law
shart	bride price
shaykh	tribal leader, chief
sunna	religious acts
suq	market
ta°awaniya	local development association
tannur	cylindrical oven used for baking bread
thawra	revolution
thumna, thuman	eighth, village cluster
°*uruf*	common law
°*usra*	family
°*uzla*	subdistrict, state administrative unit
wadi	riverbed, streambed, valley
wakil, wakala'	agent
waqf	religious endowment lands or property
za°im	Lebanese, similar to shaykh
zaka, zakat	Islamic tax
Zaydi	sect of Shi°a Islam

Bibliography

Adra, Najwa. 1982. Qabayla: The Tribal Concept in the Central Highlands of the Yemen Arab Republic. Ph.D. dissertation, Temple University.

Anis LDA Annual Report. 1978–79. Unpublished mimeograph. Sanaᶜa.

Barakat, Halim. 1977. Socioeconomic, Cultural and Personality Forces Determining Development in Arab Society. In Saad Eddin Ibrahim and Nicholas S. Hopkins (eds.), *Arab Society in Transition*. Cairo: American University.

Bardeleben, Manfred. 1973. *The Cooperative System in the Sudan*. Munich: Weltforum Verlag.

Barnett, Tony. 1977. *The Gezira Scheme: An Illusion of Development*. London: Frank Cass.

Bauer, Peter T., and Basil S. Yamey. 1957. *The Economics of Under-Developed Countries*. Chicago: University of Chicago Press.

Bryant, Coralie, and Louise G. White. 1982. *Managing Development in the Third World*. Boulder, Colo.: Westview Press.

Cantori, Louis J., and Ilya Harik (eds.). 1984. *Local Politics and Development in the Middle East*. Boulder, Colo.: Westview Press.

Carapico, S. H. 1984. The Political Economy of Self-Help: Development Cooperatives in the Yemen Arab Republic. Ph.D. dissertation, State University of New York at Binghamton.

Carroll, Thomas F. 1971. Peasant Cooperation in Latin America. In P. Worsley (ed.), *Two Blades of Grass*. Manchester: Manchester University Press.

Caton, S. 1987. Power, Persuasion and Language: A Critique of the Segmentary Model in the Middle East. *International Journal of Middle East Studies*, 19: 77–102.

Chelhod, Joseph. 1970. L'Organisation sociale au Yémen. *L'Ethnographie* 64: 61–68.

——. 1979. Social Organization in Yemen. Translated by Paul Dresch. *Darasat Yamaniya*, 2:47–62.

Chilcote, Ronald H. 1984. *Theories of Development and Underdevelopment*, Boulder, Colo.: Westview Press.

Cohen, Alvin. 1968. Externalities in the Displacement of Traditional Elites. *Economic Development and Cultural Change*, 17, no. 1: 65–75.

——. 1984. The Macroeconomic versus the Microeconomic Approach to Development: The Futility of Development Efforts as a Function of Institutional Inertia. *Economic Development and Cultural Change*, 32, no. 2: 423–30.

Cohen, John M., and David B. Lewis. 1979*a*. Capital-Surplus, Labor Short Econo-mies: Yemen as a Challenge to Rural Development Strategies. *American Jour-nal of Agricultural Economics*, 61, no. 3: (523–28).

———. 1979*b*. Review of the Literature and Analysis of Rural Development Issues in the Yemen Arab Republic, Working Note No. 6. Rural Development Commit-tee, Yemen Research Program, Center for International Studies: Cornell Uni-versity Press.

Cohen, John M., Mary Hebert, David B. Lewis, and Jon C. Swanson. 1980. Tradi-tional Organizations and Development: Yemen's Local Development Associa-tions. Local Organization, Participation and Development in the Yemen Arab Republic, Working Note No. 7. Rural Development Committee, Yemen Research Program, Center for International Studies: Cornell University.

———. 1981. Development from Below: Local Development Associations in the Yemen Arab Republic. *World Development*, 9, no. 11/12: 1039–61.

Colletta, N. J. 1979. The Sarvodaya Experience. *International Development Review*, 21, no. 3: 15–18.

Combs, Philips H. 1980. *Meeting the Basic Needs of the Rural Poor: The Inte-grated Community Based Approach*. New York: Pergamon Press.

Cooper, Charles A. 1972. *Economic Development and Population Growth in the Middle East*. New York: American Elsevier.

Crocombe, Ronald G. 1971. Social Aspects of Cooperative and Other Corporate Landholding in the Pacific Islands. In P. Worsley (ed.), *Two Blades of Grass*. Manchester: Manchester University Press.

De Vries, Egbert. 1968. A Review of Literature on Development Theory 1957–1967. *International Development Review*, 10, no. 1: 43–51. Directorate of Overseas Surveys, United Kingdom. 1979. Series YAR 50 1:50,000 contour maps.

Dobyns, Henry F., Paul Doughty, and Darold D. Lasswell (eds). 1971. *Peasants, Power and Applied Social Change: Vicos as a Model*. Beverly Hills: Sage Pub-lications.

Dore, Ronald E. 1971. Modern Cooperatives in Traditional Communities. In P. Worsley (ed.), *Two Blades of Grass* Manchester: Manchester University Press.

Dostal, Walter (revised by R. B. Serjeant and Robert Wilson). 1983. Analysis of the Sana^{c}a Market Today. In R. B. Serjeant and Ronald Lewcock (eds.), *Sana^{c}a: An Arabian Islamic City*. London: World of Islam Festival Trust.

Dresch, Paul. 1984. The Position of Shaykhs among the Northern Tribes of Yemen. *Man*, 19, no. 1: 31–49.

———. 1986. The Significance of the Course Events Take in Segmentary Systems. *American Ethnologist*, 13, no. 2: 309–24.

Eggan, Fred. 1954. Social Anthropology and the Method of Controlled Compari-son. *American Anthropologist*, 56, no. 5: 743–63.

Epstein, T. Scarlett. 1962. *Economic Development and Social Change in South India*. New York: Humanities Press.

Esman, Milton J., and Norman T. Uphoff. 1984. *Local Organizations: Intermedi-aries in Rural Development*. Ithaca: Cornell University Press.

Faris, Nabih Amin. 1938. *The Antiquities of South Arabia: Being a Translation from the Arabic with Linguistic, Geographic and Historic Notes of the Eighth Book of Al-Hamdani's al-Iklil*. Princeton: Princeton University Press.

Foster, George M. 1973. *Traditional Societies and Technological Change*. New York: Harper and Row.

Foster-Carter, A. 1976. From Rostow to Gunder Frank: Conflicting Paradigms in the Analysis of Underdevelopment. *World Development*, 4: 167–80.

Garbett, G. K. 1978. The Analysis of Social Situations. *Man*, 5, no. 2: 214–28.

Geertz, Clifford (ed.). 1979. *Meaning and Order in Moroccan Society*. Cambridge: Cambridge University Press.

Gerholm, Thomas. 1977. *Market, Mosque and Mufraj: Social Inequality in a Yemeni Town*. Stockholm: Stockholm Studies in Social Anthropology: University of Stockholm.

Gill, Richard T. 1967. *Economic Development: Past and Present*. Englewood Cliffs, N.J.: Prentice-Hall.

Glasser, Barney, and Anselm Strauss. 1967. *The Discovery of Grounded Theory: Strategies for Qualitative Research*. Chicago: Aldine.

Green, James Wyche. 1975. Local Initiative in Yemen: Exploratory Studies of Four Local Development Associations. Paper Prepared for U.S. Agency for International Development, Washington D.C.

Haaland, Gunner. 1980. Social Organization and Ecological Pressure in Southern Darfur. In G. Haaland (ed.), *Problems of Savannah Development: The Sudan Case*. Bergen, Norway: Department of Anthropology, Occasional Papers No. 19.

Hagen, Everett E. 1962. *On the Theory of Social Change*. Homewood, Ill.: Dorsey Press. (1962)

Halliday, Fred. 1974. *Arabia without Sultans*. New York: Vintage Books.

Hamer, John H. 1976. Prerequisites and Limitation in the Development of Voluntary Self-Help Associations: A Case Study and Comparison. *Anthropological Quarterly*, 49: 107–34.

Hoogstraal, Harry, and Robert Kuntz. 1952. Yemen Opens the Door to Progress. *National Geographic Magazine*, 101, no. 2: 213–44. Washington, D.C.: National Geographic Society.

Hudson, Michael C. 1968. *The Precarious Republic, Political Modernization in Lebanon*. New York: Random House.

Johnston, Bruce, and William Clark. 1982. *Redesigning Rural Development*. Baltimore: John Hopkins University Press.

Joy, Leonard J. 1971. The Analysis of Existing Social Factors Favorable to Successful Modern Cooperatives. In P. Worsley (ed.), *Two Blades of Grass*. Manchester: Manchester University Press.

Kennedy, John G. 1987. *The Flower of Paradise*. Dordrecht: D. Reidel Publishing.

Kennedy, John G., James Teague, and Lynn Fairbanks. 1980. Qat Use in North Yemen and the Problem of Addiction: A Study in Medical Anthropology. *Culture, Medicine, and Psychiatry*, 4: 311–44.

Khadr, Nirjana. 1984. Local Patterns of Leadership and the Development of the Aswan High Dam Lake. In Lewis I. Cantori and Iliya Harik (eds.), *Local Politics and Development in the Middle East*. Boulder, Colo.: Westview Press.

Khalaf, Samir. 1972. Adaptive Modernization, The Case for Lebanon. In C. Cooper and S. Alexander (eds.), *Economic Development and Population Growth in the Middle East*. New York: America Elsevier.

Khouri, Fuad. 1972. Sectarian Loyalty among Rural Migrants in Two Lebanese Suburbs: A Stage between Family and National Allegiance. In R. Antoun and I. Harik (eds.), *Rural Politics and Social Changes in the Middle East*. Bloomington: Indiana University Press.

Kuhn, Thomas. 1970. *The Structure of Scientific Revolutions*. Chicago: University of Chicago Press.

Lee, Eddy. 1981. Basic Needs Strategies: A Frustrated Response to Development from Below. In W. B. Stohr and D. R. Fraser Taylor (eds.), *Development from Above or Below*. New York: John Wiley and Sons.

Lengyel, Peter (ed.). 1971. *Approaches to the Science of Socio-economic Development*. Paris: UNESCO.

Lofgren, Oscar. 1953. *Al Hamdani-Sudarabisches Mustabih*. Uppsala: Almqvist and Wiksells Boktryckeri AB.

Mair, Lucy. 1972. *An Introduction to Social Anthropology*. New York: Oxford University Press.

Mead, Margaret. 1959. *An Anthropologist at Work: The Writings of Ruth Benedict*. Boston: Houghton Mifflin.

Meeker, Michael M. 1979. *Literature and Violence in North Arabia*. Cambridge: Cambridge University Press.

Merton, Robert K. 1949. *Social Theory and Social Structure: Towards the Codification of Theory and Research*. Glencoe, Ill.: Free Press.

Morris, Timothy C. J. 1985. Adapting to Wealth: Social Change in a Yemeni Highland Community. Ph.D. dissertation, London, School of Oriental and African Studies.

Morss, E., and D. Gow. 1985. *Implementing Rural Development Projects*. Boulder, Colo.: Westview Press.

Mundy, Martha. 1979. Women's Inheritance of Land in Highland Yemen. *Arabian Studies*, 5: 161–87.

Nash, Manning. 1959. Some Social and Cultural Aspects of Economic Development. *Economic Development and Cultural Change*, 7, no. 2: 137–50.

Niebuhr, Carsten. 1792. *Travels through Arabia*. Translated by Robert Heron. Edinburgh: R. Morison and Son.

Nurkse, R. 1953. *Problems of Capital Formation in Underdeveloped Countries*. Oxford: Basil Blackwell.

Pelto, Pertti J. 1970. *Anthropological Research, the Structure of Inquiry*. New York: Harper and Row.

Peters, Emrys. 1959. The Proliferation of Segments in the Lineage of the Bedouin of Cyrenaica. *Journal of the Royal Anthropological Institute*, 89: 29–53.

———. 1967. Some Structural Aspects of the Feud among the Camel Herding Bedouin of Cyrenaica. *Africa: Journal of the International Africa Institute*, 37, no. 3: 261–82.

Pitt, David C. 1976*a*. *Development from Below*. The Hague: Mouton Publishers.

———. 1976*b*. *The Social Dynamics of Development*. New York: Pergamon Press.

Redfield, Robert. 1956. *Peasant Society and Culture*. Chicago: University of Chicago Press.

Revri, Raman. 1983. *Catha Edulis Forsk: Geographical Dispersal, Botanical, Ecological and Agronomical Aspects with Special Reference to Yemen Arab Republic*. Göttingen: n.p.

Rihani, Ameen. 1930. *Arabian Peak and Desert*. Boston: Houghton Mifflin.

Ross, Lee Ann. 1981. An Informal Banking System: The Remittance Agents of Yemen. Local Organization, Participation and Development in the Yemen Arab Republic, Working Note No. 12. Rural Development Committee, Yemen Research Program, Center for International Studies: Cornell University.

Saunders, Robert S. 1977. Traditional Cooperation, Indigenous Peasants' Groups and Rural Development: A Look at Possibilities and Experiences. Review Paper Prepared for World Bank, Washington, D.C.

Seers, D. 1969. The Meaning of Development. *International Development Review*, 11, no. 4: 2–6.

Seibel, Hans D., and Andreas Massing. 1974. *Traditional Organizations and Economic Development*. New York: Praeger Publishers.

Serjeant, R. B. 1983. The Post-Medieval and Modern History of Sana^{c}a and the Yemen, ca. 953–1282/1515–1962. In R. B. Serjeant and Ronald Lewcock (eds.), *Sana^{c}a: An Arabian Islamic City*. London: World of Islam Festival Trust.

Serjeant, R. B., and Ronald Lewcock (eds). 1983. *Sana^{c}a, An Arabian Islamic City*. London: World of Islam Festival Trust.

Singer, H. W. 1949. Economic Progress in Underdeveloped Countries. *Social Research*, 16: 1–11.

Smith, Carol A. 1976. *Regional Analysis: Volume 1, Economic Systems*. New York: Academic Press.

Smith, M. G. 1974. *Corporations and Society*. London: Gerald Duckworth.

Steffen, H., and U. Geiser. 1977. *Preliminary Report No. 5: Databank of Yemen's Population and Housing Census 1975*. Zurich: Department of Geography, University of Zurich.

Steffen, H., et al. 1978. *Final Report on the Airphoto Interpretation Project of the Swiss Technical Cooperation Service*. Berne: Swiss Technical Cooperation Project.

Stevenson, Thomas Bruce. 1981. Kinship, Stratification and Mobility: Social Change in a Yemeni Highland Town. Ph.D. dissertation, Wayne State University.

———. 1985. *Social Change in a Yemeni Highlands Town*. Salt Lake City: University of Utah Press.

Stohr, W. B. 1981. Development from Below: The Bottom-Up and Periphery-Inward Development Paradigm. In W. B. Stohr and D. R. Fraser Taylor (eds.), *Development from Above or Below? The Dialectics of Regional Planning in Developing Countries*. New York: John Wiley and Sons.

Stohr, W. B. and D. R. Fraser Taylor (eds.). 1981. *Development from Above or Below? The Dialectics of Regional Planning in Developing Countries*. New York: John Wiley and Sons.

Stookey, Robert W. 1978. *Yemen: The Politics of the Yemen Arab Republic*. Boulder, Colo.: Westview Press.

Streeten, Paul. 1977. The Distinctive Features of a Basic Needs Approach to Development. *International Development Review*, 19, no. 3: 8–9.

Swanson, Jon C. 1979. *Emigration and Economic Development: The Case of the Yemen Arab Republic*. Boulder, Colo.: Westview Press.

Swiss Technical Cooperation. 1977. Population Distribution Administrative Division and Land Use in the Yemen Arab Republic (Map), comp. U. Geiser and H. Steffen. Berne: Swiss Technical Cooperation Service.

Tiffany, Walter. 1979. New Directions in Political Anthropology: The Use of Corporate Models for the Analysis of Political Organizations. In Lee Saton and Henri J. M. Classen (eds.), *Political Anthropology*. The Hague: Mouton Publishers.

Tutwiler, Richard. 1979. Ta^{c}awon Mahweet: Development and Social Change in a Yemeni Community. *Darasat Yemeniya*, 2: 3–14.

——. 1984. Ta°awun Mahweet: A Case Study of a Local Development Association in Highland Yemen. In Louis Cantori and Illya Harik (eds), *Local Politics and Development in the Middle East*. Boulder, Colo.: Westview Press.

——. 1987. Tribe, Tribute, and Trade: Social Class Formation in Highland Yemen. Ph.D. dissertation, State University of New York at Binghamton.

Tutwiler, Richard, and Sheila Carapico. 1981. *Yemen Agriculture and Economic Change: Case Studies of Two Highland Regions*. Sana°a: American Institute for Yemeni Studies.

Uphoff, Norman T., and Milton J. Esman. 1974. *Local Organization for Rural Development: Analysis of Asian Experience*. Ithaca, N.Y.: Rural Development Committee, Center for International Studies.

Varisco, Daniel Martin. 1986. On the Meaning of Chewing: The Significance of Qat in the Yemen Arab Republic. *International Journal of Middle East Studies*, 18, no. 1: 1–13.

Wallerstein, Immanuel. 1974. *The Modern World System: Capitalist Agriculture and the Origins of the European World-Economy in the Sixteenth Century*. New York: Academic Press.

Wenner, Manfred. 1967. *Modern Yemen (1918–1966)*. Baltimore: Johns Hopkins Press.

Wiarda, Howard J. 1983. Toward a Nonethnocentric Theory of Development: Alternative Conceptions from the Third World. *Journal of Developing Areas*, 17: 433–52.

Widstrand, Carl G. (ed.). 1972. *African Cooperatives and Efficiency*. Uppsala: Scandinavian Instistute of African Studies.

Wolf, Eric. 1966. *Peasants*. New York: Prentice-Hall.

Worsley, Peter. 1971. *Two Blades of Grass*. Manchester: Manchester University Press.

Yemen Arab Republic Government (YARG). 1971. The Permanent Constitution of the Yemen Arab Republic. *Middle East Journal*, 25: 389–401.

——. 1976*b*. *The First Five Year Plan*. Sana°a: Central Planning Organization.

——. 1976*b*. *National Health Programme 1976/77–1981/82*. Sana°a: Ministry of Health.

——. 1977. *Yemen Arab Republic Statistical Yearbook*. Sana°a: Central Planning Organization.

——. 1980. *Sample Agriculture Census of Dhamar and al-Hudayda Governorates* (in Arabic). Sana°a: Ministry of Agriculture.

——. 1981. *Statistical Yearbook of the Tenth Year*. Sana°a: Central Planning Organization.

——. 1982. *The Second Five Year Plan*. Sana°a: Central Planning Organization.

——. 1983*a*. *Final Results of the 1981 Population Census* (in Arabic). Census conducted by the Confederation of Yemen Development Associations (CYDA). Sana°a: Central Planning Organization.

——. 1983*b*. *Statistical Yearbook of the Twelfth Year*. Sana°a: Central Planning Organization.

Young, Frank W., and M. Hebert, and J. Swanson. 1981. The Ecological Context of Local Development in Yemen. Local Organization, Participation, and Development in the Yemen Arab Republic, Working Note No. 13. Rural Development Committee, Yemen Research Program, Center for International Studies: Cornell University.

Zabara, Mohammed A. 1982. *Traditionalism vs. Modernity*. New York: Praeger Publishers.

Index

Rural electrification, 49, 75–77. See also Rural areas, consumerism in

Savings, cash, levels of, 50–51
Sayyids, status of, in Jibal Rayma, 113, 115
Schools and education, 62, 65–66, 70–72, 78–79, 156, 162
Sectarian allegiance, 14
Sectarian politics, 161–62
Sectarianism, religious, 159, 160–64, 184 chap 7 nn2–5; rural development and, 10–11, 157–58, 159–60, 167–68; sociopolitical institutions and, 12–13, 159–66
Security measures, tribal, 127–28
Settlement patterns, 27–29, 44, 99
Shafiᶜi religious sect, 157–64, 165
Sharecropping, 23, 110, 115
Shaykh, 95, 152; political factionalism of, 139, 141–44; relationship of, to Anis tribe, 100, 108–12; status of, in Anis, 154–55; status of, in Jibal Rayma, 106, 113–18, 130
Shiᶜa Islam, 157, 158
Shopkeepers, 23, 26, 58–59, 60, 169
Social relationships, in development and change, 9–13, 14, 93, 95–97, 99, 100–101, 106–7, 123, 151, 152, 154–55, 156, 168–69
Sociopolitical structures, 6, 122, 123–25, 183 n10; in Anis, 14, 134–38, 147–48, 149; in Anis tribe, 100–105, 107–12, 118–19, 125–29, 132; description of, 93–100; in Jibal Rayma, 14, 105–8, 112–18, 119, 129–32, 138–45; of local development associations, 124–25, 133–45; rural development and, 9–14, 167, 168; tribe and religious sects in, 12–13, 93, 122–24, 125–29, 159–66
Subdistrict, description of, 98–99
Subprovince, description of, 95, 97–98
Sudanese Gezira scheme, 3
Sunni Islam, 157

Taxation, 2, 53, 66, 85, 89–91, 98–99, 113, 114, 115, 129, 158–59, 173, 178 n4, 182 n10
Teachers, shortage of, 62
Terrace agriculture, 18, 20, 21; abandonment of, 54, 56, 83
Territorial boundaries, friction over, 102–5
Tihama, the, 7, 17, 27, 53–54
Tribal confederations, 94, 100, 126
Tribal law, 109
Tribal membership, 14; alliances within, 94–95, 101–5
Tribal system: development and, 10–11, 147, 150–51, 167, 169; leadership in, 152; religious sects and, 158–59, 164–65; security measures in, 127–28; sociopolitical institutions and, 12–13, 159–66
Tribal values, in rural development, 147, 150–51
Tribe: description of, 94; structure of, 93, 95, 97, 122–24, 183 n5
Tribe, Anis, 98, 125–29, 133, 147–48
Tribes, independence of, 63
Tribesmen: attitude toward marketplace, 52, 53; egalitarianism among, 155–57

Urban areas, migration to, 47
USAID projects, 77

Villages: Anis, 100, 101; description of, 99; Jibal Rayma, 107

Wages, in rural areas, 48
Water storage and supply systems, 18, 21–22, 55, 65–66, 67, 75–77
Women. See Division of labor, agricultural; Marketplace, women in

Yemen Arab Republic, creation of, 1
Yemen, highland, subsistence of, 7–8

Zaydi religious sect, 157–64, 165